Spiritual
Counsel
to the Young

J.K. Popham

OLD PATHS
gOSPEL PRESS

P.O. Box 318 • Choteau, MT 59422
Phone or Fax: (406) 466-2311

Paperback edition issued 1977
by Baker Book House Company
ISBN: 0-8010-7020-1
Formerly published under the title,
Letters to the Young, the chapters
are a collection of monthly letters
which appeared in "Friendly Companion."

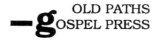

OLD PATHS
OSPEL PRESS

P.O. Box 318 • Choteau, MT 59422
Phone or Fax: (406) 466-2311

AUTHOR'S NOTE.

❧

MY part in the appearance of this little book was to consent to it. The writing of the letters was a serious business preceded by prayer, under a sense of the importance of providing suitable reading for the young. They are now followed by prayer that a divine blessing may rest on them.

J. K. POPHAM.

CONTENTS.

❧

LETTERS TO THE YOUNG

Types, Figures, Patterns, etc.

1.

My dear young Friends,—When reading the inspired book of Ezra lately, I was struck with several prominent points in that remarkable relation of the return of the so long banished people; and there appeared some instruction in them to which I desire, by the Lord's help, to draw your attention.

I. The FIRST POINT is the *punctual* and *exact fulfilment of the threatened punishment, in and by banishment and captivity,* and

II. *The promise of restoration of Israel from Babylon at the end of seventy years.*

Now, it will be an excellent exercise for you all, to look up the Scriptures which threaten a sinful and sinning nation with solemn judgment, banishment, and seventy years' captivity. Then come to Ezra, and he will tell you of God's faithfulness, both in the captivity and the return of the captives. " Now in the first year of Cyrus, king of Persia, that the word of the Lord, by the mouth of Jeremiah, might be fulfilled, the Lord stirred up the spirit of Cyrus, king of Persia, that he made a proclamation throughout all his kingdom, and put it also in writing, saying, Thus saith Cyrus, king of Persia, the Lord God of heaven hath given me all the kingdoms of the earth: and He hath charged me to build Him an house at Jerusalem, which is in Judah," etc. (Ezra i.). How often would some of the " ancient men," who lived through all those seventy weary years, have thought of the warnings, and threatenings, and exhortations of that mournful and mourning prophet, Jeremiah, to whom they might have listened, and whom they saw apprehended, but whose awful words they

heeded not. Oh, young readers, it is a solemn thing to
sin against and provoke a jealous God; to turn away
from, and despise, His Word. He says, " Be sure your
sin will find you out." When men, wrapped up in
themselves, and secure in their own ways, say, " Peace
and safety; then sudden destruction cometh upon them."
The false prophets who promised peace and safety to
sinful, blind, wayward Jerusalem, found, with that
whole city, that the word of the Lord was sure. In all
who die in sin, Solomon's words will be found terribly
and eternally true: " Rejoice, O young man, in thy
youth; and let thy heart cheer thee in the days of thy
youth, and walk. in the ways of thine heart, and in the
sight of thine eyes: but, know thou, that for all these
things God will bring thee into judgment " (Eccles. xi.
9). I think it is Bunyan who says those are a " solemn
irony." For every idle word you must give an account.
So far the threatening word. Then, on the other hand,
when any poor sinner finds conviction working, and
conscience telling him that he is in the way to hell, and
deserves to be there; that he is in bondage to sin and
Satan; that God is against him; many sad hours are
spent in secret, confessing sin and seeking pardon and
salvation, then such a person shall find the " sure mercies of David." Whoever perished seeking Him, who,
in their hearts, by the Spirit's unperceived operation,
is saying, " Seek ye My face " ? The word is established in the very heavens, that they that seek shall
find. Out of every prison will the great Deliverer call
each prisoner, saying with almighty effectual voice,
" Show yourself."
This, then, is the first point I observed in Ezra.
There is an exact performance of the mercy promised
to all the seed; the Lord remembers for each one His
holy covenant. Notice this remarkable truth: " Heaven
and earth shall pass away, but the word of the Lord
abideth for ever."
God bless you all with His saving mercy.
Your affectionate friend,
Brighton, May, 1920.   J. K. POPHAM.

2.

My dear young Friends,—In my last letter I drew your attention to the fulfilment of God's merciful promise to restore His people to their own land at the end of their seventy years' captivity, as seen in the book of Ezra. The holy, wise, and mighty providence of God shines in all Spirit-opened eyes in the proclamation of Cyrus, a stranger to the covenants of promise. The God of heaven thus speaks of him: " I have raised him up in righteousness, and I will direct all his ways; he shall build My city, and he shall let go My captives, not for price nor reward, saith the Lord of hosts " (Isa. xlv. 13). Thus came back to their own land a remnant of the twelve tribes. The long estrangement, and the wars between the ten tribes and the two came to an end; the dispersion led to re-union (Ezra vi. 17; viii. 35; Acts xxvi. 7; Jas. i. 1; 1 Chron. ix. 1—3). Often chastisement leads to mercy.

In this letter I want you to watch the returning captives. They do not all return at the same time. i. Numbers return with Zerubbabel (Ezra ii. 2). The names of the heads of the families are given, and the numbers of the families. Here are one or two interesting points, interesting chiefly because they are types. 1. The leader, Zerubbabel, was a type of Christ (Zech. iv. 7—9). Christ is the Leader and Commander of His people (Isa. lv. 4); also the divine Builder (1 Cor. iii. 9). With Zerubbabel was Jeshua—Joshua—the high priest (Hag. i. 1), who also was a type of Christ. He combines both these types in Himself. As High Priest He offered Himself without spot to God; and as the Leader He goes before His sheep (Jno. x. 4; Ps. xxiii. 1).

ii. After the return of all the families with Zerubbabel, their genealogies were examined, an important point with Jews. And with the fact comes a spiritual point. In all their life and history the Jews were typical. In your reading of their history keep this in mind; it will explain much. The long lists of names are not without their meaning, their pointings. In this second chapter there were some who could not produce their genealogy, and so they were, as polluted, put from the priesthood (v. 62). This does not prove the ecclesiasticism which Church people contend for, but points to the solemn importance of having an evidence of being born again of an incorruptible seed, and belonging to a chosen generation, and the royal priesthood Peter speaks of (1 Peter ii. 9). But how shall the point be decided? Many will be saying they cannot decide the doubtful case. In the case before us, the decision was to be in the hands of "a priest with Urim and with Thummim." Urim and Thummim are thought to mean light and truth. By them God communicated His mind to the priest. Does not this point to Christ, the great High Priest of our profession? He is the Light and the Truth. If, therefore, a poor sinner is drawing anxious breath with respect to his new, heavenly birth, the decision must be given by Him; He can say, and He only, "Thou art Mine."

iii. Some years after this "Ezra went up from Babylon: and he was a ready scribe in the law of Moses" (vii. 1—6). Of his journey we have an interesting account; it was a long and arduous journey. He started on the first day of the first month, and reached Jerusalem on the first day of the fifth month (v. 9), and found gratitude welling up in his heart for his safe journey and for the liberal provision which God put into the heart of the king for the beautifying of the house of the Lord in Jerusalem. The danger and difficulties of the tedious journey are to be imagined by the course Ezra took with respect to them (ch. viii. 21—23), but that they must have been considerable is clear from the king's willingness to provide a convoy. But the servant of the Lord would not compromise his Master's honour, would not share it with the king (v. 22). The returning captives will depend on their God. Ezra's faith is honoured (vs. 21—23).

What prompted and animated these men, Zerubbabbel, Jeshua, Ezra, and Nehemiah, to leave ease, and face

laborious journeys, dangers, and opposition? Doubtless
the Spirit of the living God. They were His chosen
instruments to bring back His long-banished people.
His good Spirit dwelt in them; so they laboured and
suffered. They were typical men. They set the altar
upon its bases, and offered burnt offerings thereon, they
built the temple, and repaired the wall of the city, all
in troublous times. They were men wondered at and
mocked. And their example helped the people. So it
is in the church of Christ, and will be to the end. God
has His own instruments; these He indwells, teaches
them what to do, and enables them to do it. The
sacrifice first, the acceptance of the people first, then
their work in the Lord, which they are assured is not in
vain (1 Cor. xv. 58).

God bless you, my friends.

Your affectionate friend,

Brighton, June, 1920.   J. K. POPHAM.

3.

My dear young Friends,—Having directed your attention to two special points, noticeable in connection with
the return of the Israelites from their long captivity,
in the May and June numbers of our " Friendly Companion," I want you to follow me while I notice a *third*
point in the same connection. Probably no one could
read carefully either Ezra or Nehemiah without being
struck with their constant seeking of God in all their
difficulties. It was not for nothing that very early on
their return the altar was set upon his bases, and the
people kept the feast of the tabernacles, and afterwards
offered the continual burnt offering. Thus the ordained
way of seeking God was opened. This is a type of
Christ, and His opening a new and living way to God
(Heb. x. 19—21). Though they had not the altar and
burnt offering in their long and tedious journey to Jerusalem, yet both Ezra and Nehemiah in their difficulties
sought the Lord in the living way, for He was entreated
of them (Ezra viii. 23; ix.; Neh. i. 11; iv. 4; vi. 9;
ix. 9). We see in these passages how, when God

restores people, true worship is re-established: reading, confession and prayer become common characteristics among them. This is a true mark of a child of God in all time. Indwelling sin, temptations, trials in providence, have ever been best dealt with and borne by prayer. Rehum, the Chancellor, and Shimshai, the scribe, may write a letter against Jerusalem to Artaxerxes, king of Persia, and later Sanballat the Horonite, and Tobiah the servant, the Ammonite, and Geshem the Arabian, may laugh to scorn the weary builders, but the Lord opened His eyes and looked on His afflicted ones, and opened His ears and heard the cry of the men, His banished ones, whom He had brought home again. For who shall let when the God of heaven arises for the help of His feeble Jews? Ahithophel gives good counsel, but it could not materialise when God designed to defeat it. David's prayer was answered. Jeremiah's enemies could shut him in prison, even in the low dungeon, but they could not shut out his prayer from heaven, nor prevent his God from drawing near to him and saying, "Fear not." Hezekiah's enemy—death— threatened him, even the Lord spoke the solemn death-sentence, but prayer—to use Hart's words—" brought the recanting prophet back, and turned the mind of God."

Perhaps this important point will touch a responsive chord in some of your hearts, and even be the means of stirring you to seek the Lord more. God grant it may be so for your good. It is clear from the Scriptures generally, and in the cases before us, that prayer is a weapon for the feeble; it pleases God; it brings much good. (See Ps. xviii.)

The Spirit of God make you praying people!

So prays, your affectionate friend,

Brighton, July, 1920.　　　　　　　J. K. POPHAM.

4.

My dear young Friends,—Let me introduce to your notice the Vine, and the figurative uses the Holy Ghost makes of it in Holy Scripture. Everything God makes

mention of in His Word is worthy of notice, so I make
no apology for drawing your attention to it, even though
you may say, "What is the vine tree more than any
tree, or than a branch which is among the trees of the
forest? Shall wood be taken thereof to do any work?
or will men take a pin of it to hang any vessel thereon?" (Ezek. xv. 2, 3.) The culture of the vine is
carried on in many parts of the world, extending from
about the twenty-first to the fiftieth degree of north
latitude. It thrives in America, in South Africa, and
in Australia. Quite early it is mentioned in Scripture
(Gen. ix. 20), and again, by means of a dream, we see it
as grown in Egypt (Gen. xl. 11). And we may judge
that it was familiar to Israel when they were in captivity there, for they murmured at the loss of it when
they were in the wilderness (Num. xx. 5).

The land of promise, too, "the good land," was a land
"of vineyards" (Deut. vi. 11). The grapes of Eshcol
were an evidence of the wonderful fruitfulness of their
future inheritance. "Bunches of grapes weighing from
6 lb. to 7 lb. are said to be by no means uncommon, and
Sir Moses Montefiore said he saw a bunch a yard long.
It was probably such a bunch that the spies carried
betwixt two, though it might have been carried in that
way to keep it from being injured."*

Now there seems no reason against believing that
God, who knows all His works from the beginning of
the world, primarily intended the Vine to be a figure.
i. It is a figure of Christ. "I am the true Vine" (Jno.
xv. 1). In this figure there is more intended than the
union of the branches with the stock; the wonderful
fruitfulness of the Lord of life is set forth. What do
His people need that He has not to bestow? More
abundant life, perfect justification, unsullied holiness, a
filling with the fruits of righteousness, an abounding in
all good works, power to do all things to the glory of
God, whether we eat or drink, and a meetness to be
partakers of the inheritance of the saints in light; all

* Gadsby's Wanderings, p. 458.

these precious fruits grow only on the true Vine. ii. It is a figure of the union of all the people of God with Christ, and their dependence on Him for all the fruit they are to bear to the glory of God (*vs.* 5, 8).

iii. The vine is a figure of fruitless professors who are prolific in false religion. "Israel is an empty vine, he bringeth forth fruit unto himself: according to the multitude of his fruit he hath increased the altars; according to the goodness of his land they have made goodly images" (Hos. x. 1). An abundance of religion, but no fruit to the glory of God. God had bestowed much labour on that covenant people; "wherefore when I looked that it should bring forth grapes, brought it forth wild grapes?" (Isa. v. 1, 4.) The more the people increased in wealth by the providence of God, the more they went from Him, and poured out His wealth to idols (Ezek. xvi.).

iv. The vine is a figure of the extreme lengths of wickedness to which men, cast off by God, will run. Israel, turned into the degenerate plant of a strange vine, given up to their enemies for punishment, became unto God even as the vine of Sodom, and of the fields of Gomorrah; their grapes were grapes of gall, their clusters are bitter, their wine is the poison of dragons, and the cruel venom of asps (Deut. xxxii. 32, 33; Jer. ii. 21). Josephus says that the ashes of the five cities still "grow in their fruits, which fruits have a colour as if they were fit to be eaten, but if you pluck them with your hands they dissolve into smoke and ashes." Nothing but smoke and ashes will emanate from fallen man, and when an individual or a nation is given up to hardness and blindness, then the most violent wickedness shows itself. Thus, the sins of Sodom represent the worst forms of human wickedness. Josephus describes the sins of the Jews before their ruin by the Romans: "There was no act of wickedness that was not committed; nor can anyone imagine anything so bad that they did not do; endeavouring, publicly as well as privately, to excel one another both in impiety towards God and injustice to their neighbours."

Here we may ask, "Does England answer to the 'degenerate plant of a strange vine'?" She has prospered prodigiously, and as she has increased in wealth, so she has multiplied altars to Popery, to Higher Criticism, to pleasure, to profanity. Must not the crown fall from our head? woe unto us for that we have sinned.

Consider the above things, and may God give you all an understanding heart.

Your affectionate friend,
Brighton, February, 1921.   J. K. POPHAM.

5.

My dear young Friends,—When thinking about my next letter to you, and asking the Lord to guide me in the matter, the subject of "Patterns" came into my mind, and it was at once attractive, and seemed a likely subject to interest you, and one which might, by the blessing of God, be profitable. So that is to be the theme of this letter. Of course, it will appeal to you as a thing of common and universal need. You will see at once all things of a given size and form are made after a pattern, or form. A pattern, therefore, is a model or design proposed for imitation. It determines the work to be done. The world abounds with models. The Patent Office, no doubt, possesses innumerable quantities of patents. All of them are supposed to be minutely described; any looseness of description might lead to serious consequences and litigation, as the law is very stringent with regard to infringements. But registered patents are only for a time; with the expiration of the legal time the patent is no longer a patent, the particular property lapses, and anyone can imitate the patent, or improve on it, or it may die and be forgotten.

But the first pattern I am bringing before you is a divine one, and that which was made after it is of infinite importance, and of undying interest and blessing. It is the *Tabernacle.* Its size, form, materials, and furniture were all minutely given by God to His faithful servant Moses. It was to be His own House. Nothing was left to the discretion of the builder. The divine injunction was strict (Ex. xxv. 9, 40; xxvi. 30). Moses saw all that wonderful structure, it was written in his heart and on his memory. And lest any errors or mistakes should be made by his subordinates, the Lord, who is never lacking in instruments for the accomplishment of His works, called and qualified Bezaleel and his helpers, and gave them extraordinary wisdom, understanding, and skill (Ex. xxxi. 2—11; xxxv. 30—35). Thus did He provide for the most accurate execution of His beautiful design, or pattern. These good men were able to understand whatever Moses told or drew for them. It was necessary it should be so. For the Tabernacle was for God's residence among the chosen people. His glory was to be within it. It was to be the centre of Israel's whole life. The measure of their obedience and disobedience was the Tabernacle; as they "served" it they were accepted, as they grew weary of it they were regarded as being weary of the Lord. All their worship, wisdom, beauty, and strength were in the Tabernacle. Thither must the tribes go up to their God; thence should they return to their families with blessings. In famine, sickness, captivity, their mournful returns in confession and prayers were to be towards the house built for the Name of their God. This was the first reason as given by the Lord for the erection of His house: "And let them make Me a sanctuary; that I may dwell among them" (Ex. xxv. 8). But this was a type, a clear cut type. It was "a figure for the time then present" in which there was nothing made perfect. By it the Holy Ghost signified that the way into the holiest of all was not yet made manifest. It was a removable thing. It only remained till the Seed should come to whom the promise was made, the "One greater than the temple." When He came there was no room, no use for the pattern; its removal was necessary. For the type and its antitype cannot co-exist in the same place, at the same time. The "shadow" flees away when the "body" is present, which is Christ (Col. ii. 17).

After the service of the Tabernacle, very real and of

immense importance to Israel, comes its *typical* meaning.
It was not an end. Beneath it, and beyond it, lay a
truth, a glory, of which it was " a shadow, but not the
very image," but of which the faith of every gracious
Jew got some distant view—" some better thing," in
which all the families of the earth shall be blessed (Gen.
xii. 3). Of Him the Tabernacle and its furniture spoke,
even the Lord Jesus Christ. He is the " minister of the
Sanctuary, and of the true Tabernacle, which the Lord
pitched, and not man " (Heb. viii. 2). The lovely
pattern showed to Moses, according to which he made
the Tabernacle, was a typical picture, a gracious pre-
diction of the Son of Man, Jesus. For His only-begotten Son the eternal Father prepared a body. In that
sacred body " dwelleth all the fulness of the Godhead "
(Col. ii. 9). So Christ Himself said to the Pharisees:
" But I say unto you, That in this place there is One
greater than the temple " (Matt. xii. 6; Jno. ii. 19, 21).
In the Tabernacle were no windows. When the
framework of boards was erected, the roof was of curtains falling over all. Curtains composed the roof. All
the light it had was within itself. To this Christ
answers exactly. He receives no light from the world.
He is the light of the world, and whosoever believeth
in Him has the light of life, and does not walk in
darkness. Thus He answers to the wonderful candle-
stick which was " all one beaten work of pure gold."
Space, and the fact that I am writing only a letter,
forbids my describing particularly the furniture of the
Tabernacle—the laver, the altar of burnt offering, the
table of shewbread, the altar of incense, the holiest of
all, in which was the ark containing the law, the golden
mercy-seat, and the cherubims looking upon it. Each
of the above had its use, and its deep that couched
beneath. Each typified in some way the Lord Jesus.
The laver may have signified the washing of regeneration and renewing of the Holy Ghost, and also the
daily cleansing of the hands and feet (Titus iii. 5; Jno.
xiii. 10). The altar of burnt offering sets forth the
blessed altar whereof every child of God has a grace-

given right to eat (Heb. xiii. 10). The table of shew-bread says Christ is the Bread of life. The altar of incense teaches the infinitely meritorious sacrifice of the Lord Jesus by which the Saviour entered into heaven, having obtained eternal redemption, and by which His purchased people enter with the boldness of faith into the holiest. This is the new and living way, which He hath consecrated for us through the veil, that is to say, His flesh. In the holiest of all the Lord meets with His people, His suppliants, and communes with them from the mercy-seat.

Perhaps this little skeleton sketch may make the reading of the pattern showed to Moses in the mount more interesting to you. Oh, if the Spirit were pleased to open your eyes to see that "it is not possible that the blood of bulls and of goats should take away sins" (Heb. x. 4), you would then desire to see beauty, glory, and desirableness in what follows in the same chapter: "For by one offering He hath perfected for ever them that are sanctified" (ver. 14).

Only one pattern have I brought before you in this letter; it was my intention to show you others, but perhaps it is best that this glorious one, and a little of its typical character, should occupy the whole of it. God bless you.

Your affectionate friend,

Brighton, May, 1927.   J. K. POPHAM.

6.

My dear young Friends,—I wonder if the reading of my last letter was made really useful to you, if the Spirit of Christ led any of you to look beyond the type and caused you to see the Anti-type, Jesus the Son of God. Probably you sing with others the most true words:

"None but Jesus,
Can do helpless sinners good."

Now to *feel* we are sinners is to be prepared to hear of, seek after, and find Him. It is good to be well

informed in the letter of Scripture, but it is not good
to *rest satisfied* with, and in, that information.

" True religion's more than notion,
Something must be known and felt."

And that something may be compressed into two mighty,
profound words, words which have eternity in them, an
eternity of woe and of bliss. When the foolish and wicked
fashions of this life, and the world shall have passed
away, when all men shall be standing before the righteous Judge of all the earth to " receive the things done
in his body, according to all that he hath done, whether
it be good or bad," then you who read these lines, and I
who have written them, shall be there.   Books and *A
Book* will be opened.   Books of sins and the names of
the doers of the sins, and the Book of life will be
opened.   Oh, to have our names in that Book!

My usually busy life has been more than usually full
since my last letter was written to you, and this note is
all I am able to write for June.   It is written and sent
to you with desires for your good.   May God bless you
in this world, and in the world to come.

Your affectionate friend,
Brighton, June, 1927.   J. K. POPHAM.

7.

My dear young Friends,—" Known unto God are all
His works, from the beginning of the world," and all
that He purposed to do among and with men.   Whatever He is permitting to be done, and Himself is doing
in this the evening of this world's sinful, sinning life,
and in the slumbering church, was in His eternal mind.
From the beginning until now, by degrees, and by
various and strange instruments, He has been speaking
and working.   In His work in the calling of sinners,
He says, " I the Lord will hasten it in His time."   Woe
to the people that say, " Let Him make speed and
hasten His work that we may see it; and let the counsel
of the Holy One of Israel draw nigh and come, that we
may know it."   Only *by faith*—His own merciful gift

to some men—can any *wait* on Him, and for Him. To
his own blind, impatient self, man is always turning.
In heart all say to God, " Depart from us, for we
desire not the knowledge of Thy ways." However, the
Almighty is undisturbed. " He is in one mind, and who
can turn Him ? and what His soul desireth even that
He doeth." Among His works, His communications to
men will be found not to be the least. By them He
has made known His mind concerning His worship,
what we call religion. " God, who at sundry times and
in divers manners spake in time past unto the fathers,
hath in these last days spoken unto us by His Son, by
whom He made the worlds. Who being the brightness
of His glory, and the express image of His Person, and
upholding all things by the word of His power, when
He had by Himself purged our sins, sat down on the
right hand of the Majesty on high." Now before this
glorious God-Man appeared, God spoke and taught
Israel in divers manners and in various degrees, chiefly
and permanently during the whole of that dispensation,
by types. The teaching by types is called typology. If
I might coin a term I would call it *prophecy by figure.*
For the Levitical types were prophetic. They all said,
" There is One to come, of whom, and of His great work
and the fruit of it, and the acceptableness of it, and the
glory of it, we figure out to you to whom the Lord has
not given an heart to perceive, and eyes to see, and
ears to hear, unto this day." It was then an unutter-
able judgment on men who heard but understood not,
who saw but perceived not. Seven hundred years after
Moses, the same judicial blindness fell on the same
nation (Isa. vi. 9, 10). And on multitudes the self-
same judgment fell in the days of Christ on the earth,
hence the proud question, " Are we blind also ? " And
who will deny that the righteous Lord, who will not,
cannot, do iniquity, has said, " Make the heart of the
(Modernists) fat, and make their ears heavy, and shut
their eyes; lest they see with their eyes, and hear with
their ears, and understand with their heart, and convert,
and be healed " ? But *some* hear. For Christ was sent

and anointed to reveal and preach His Father's righteousness, and faithfulness, and salvation, and lovingkindness in the great congregation; and "to preach good tidings unto the meek, to bind up the brokenhearted, to proclaim liberty to the captives, and the opening of the prison to them that are bound." For about one thousand and five hundred years the Lord taught Israel by " a shadow of good things to come, and not the very image of things." For, generally, a type is, in Scripture, a person or object, used as a model, or pattern (Heb. viii. 5). Adam was the figure of Him that was to come (Rom. v. 14). The terrible consequence of unbelief and rebellion is set before all who read the Bible, as " an ensample " or type of the just anger of God (1 Cor. x. 11).

Now I want you to consider one type or figure of Christ, viz., *Melchisedec*. I won't trouble you with the conjectures, theories, and mismanagement of this type, in which many men have indulged. As is said of Adam that he was the figure of Him that was to come, so it is true of Melchisedec, he was a figure of our High Priest. Three facts concerning Melchisedec shall suffice us. i. *That he was a man.* " And Melchisedec King of Salem brought forth bread and wine; and he was the priest of the Most High God." ii. *That his pedigree, or parentage, is to all men unknown*—" Without father, without mother, without descent, having neither beginning of days, nor end of life; but made like unto the Son of God; abideth a priest continually." The withholding of his pedigree, birth and death, is by the wisdom of God, to forefigure the eternity of the Son of God, our Great High Priest. iii. *That he filled two great offices.* (a) That of a king—king of Salem; (b) That of a priest—priest of the Most High God. We should not err if we regarded Melchisedec as a type of the Prince of peace. " Of the increase of His government and peace there shall be no end." But the Holy Ghost sets him forth in the one typical, striking, initial, all-important office of priest: " The Lord hath sworn, and will not repent, Thou art a priest for ever after the order of Melchisedec " (Ps. cx. 4). The exalted position of Melchisedec, as the priest of the Most High God, is a type of the Great High Priest of our profession. " Now consider how great this man was, unto whom even the patriarch Abraham gave the tenth of the spoils. And without all contradiction the less is blessed of the better." Thus we see in type that, however great and exalted in position a person may be, whenever the Priest of the Most High God meets him with the bread of His own body, and the wine of His own blood, " without all contradiction the less is blessed of the better." It is worthy of our best attention that the Lord Jesus is not a priest after the order of Aaron, but after the order of Melchisedec; that Aaron was inducted into the office of high priest without an oath, but Christ " with an oath by Him that said unto Him, The Lord sware and will not repent, Thou art a Priest for ever after the order of Melchisedec." This divine oath secures an unchangeable Priesthood to the Lord, and makes Him a Surety of a better testament. Aaron, as the high priest under the law, went once a year into the holiest, not without blood. Jesus " our Forerunner is for us entered, made an High Priest for ever after the order of Melchisedec," " having by one offering perfected for ever them that are sanctified." And therefore there is a new and living way opened into the holiest by the blood of Jesus, and a High Priest over the house of God. So every sensible sinner, under the sentence of death by the law, is thus directed to " draw near with a true heart in full assurance of faith," full assurance of the sufficiency of the atonement. And the High Priest graciously says, " Come unto Me all ye that labour and are heavy laden, and I will give you rest."

God grant that you may be brought to know your need of the great High Priest, made a High Priest after the order of Melchisedec. So prays,

Your affectionate friend,

Brighton, June, 1928.   J. K. POPHAM.

The Character of God.

1.

My dear young Friends,—I wonder how many, if any of you, have been led to consider the character of the eternal God. In Him you all live, and move, and have your being. You are dependent on Him for health and every comfort you enjoy. Is it true of all of you that God is not in all your thoughts; that you are in the same condition as the heathen who have no Bible, no teaching of it, no ministry of truth, unless you are born again? As unbelievers, you are under condemnation. Towards you, as in the above state and condition, the character of God is that of a just Judge, who will by no means clear the guilty, whose awful word concerning you is, "Cursed is every one that continueth not in all things which are written in the book of the law to do them." Of God it is written, "He is the Rock; His work is perfect; for all His ways are judgment: a God of truth and without iniquity, just and right is He" (Deut. xxxii. 4). The glory of God in the law is great and everlasting. It is called the ministration of death, and is glorious (2 Cor. iii. 7). If you are able to keep the whole law, and can say of the commandments what the young man said to Christ, that you have kept them, and yet "offend in one point, you are guilty of all" (James ii. 10). You have made a rent in the whole law and will be judged as guilty and deserving death. In this is the most awful, just, and glorious character of Jehovah. Punishment in hell is *just* punishment, because it is God's punishment. Holiness is in His infliction of vindicatory justice. God grant to you a conviction of this by the Holy Ghost, then you will *feel* sin, and *feel* the just sentence of the law, and judge yourselves, and feel guilty, and sink low in fear, and dark forebodings, and the terror of the Lord will fill your hearts. O how just and right and glorious will God appear to you! You will know His character. But the revelation of divine glory in the ministration of death is only partial, and in relation to the church is to be done away (2 Cor. iii. 11). The greater, the excelling glory, is the gospel. In the ministration of the Spirit forgiveness, justification, and sanctification are made known in the heart, and then the fuller character of God is known. He is loved because He is love. He speaks in love, deals in love with all to whom He shows Himself in the glorious gospel of Christ. Christ is to them the brightness of His Father's glory, the express image of His Person. He becomes to them the Shepherd and Bishop. He is the Fountain of life in them, the Wisdom of God and the power of God. How we need Him! No pastures to feed in without His leading (Ps. xxiii.); no Bishop to rule, no water of life to refresh, no wisdom to walk; no strength to keep the faith, without the Lord Jesus. Here is the wonderful character of God. It is a river of pleasures for evermore. Nothing good can be found in our fallen nature; all good and only good in the Lord Jesus Christ. What a wonder of eternal love it will be if you know God, or rather, are known of God! In such a case all will be well for ever and ever. Sin, Satan, the world and mortality will no more burden, afflict, and wound. O to reach heaven and to know even as we are known! That such may be your blessedness and mine, prays,

Your affectionate friend,

Brighton, July, 1933.   J. K. POPHAM.

2.

My dear young Friends,—In beautiful language Holy Scripture tells of the constant change—succession of seasons, the passing away of men, and the abiding of the earth. "One generation passeth away and another generation cometh; but the earth abideth for ever. The sun ariseth, and the sun goeth down, and hasteth to the place where he arose. The wind goeth toward the south, and turneth about unto the north; it whirleth about continually, and the wind returneth again according to his circuits. All the rivers run into the sea; yet the sea is not full; unto the place from whence the rivers come, thither they return again" (Eccles. i. 4—7).

Vicissitude is also stamped on man while here: "All things are full of labour; man cannot utter it; the eye is not satisfied with seeing, nor the ear filled with hearing" (ver. 8). All this were gloomy in the extreme to the children of God, but for the revelation which He has condescended to give in the Word of God of Himself. This was the Psalmist's comfort in the affliction that was on him, and the prospect of death, and the ultimate perishing of the earth and the heavens, the work of His hands: "They shall perish, but Thou shalt endure: yea, all of them shall wax old as doth a garment; as a vesture shalt Thou change them, and they shall be changed. But Thou art the same, and Thy years shall have no end" (Ps. cii. 24—27). The unchangeableness of God is the Rock of ages. And this is mercifully reflected in His Word: "For ever, O Lord, Thy word is settled in heaven." "Heaven and earth shall pass away, but My words shall not pass away" (Ps. cxix. 89; Matt. xxiv. 35). Thus the immutability of the Word of God is His own unchangeable nature. His promise to Abraham He confirmed by an oath, and He swore by His own Being because there was no greater (Heb. v. 14—17).

Now the immutability of God, as set forth by Holy Scripture, acts on two very different classes of people. (1) The ungodly unbelievers, professors of religion. Read very carefully Num. xiii. and xiv., and Heb. iii. and iv. These solemn passages of Scripture show the terrible position and condition of professors of God's holy Name, while in works they deny Him. And those chapters are as true and as descriptive of many to-day as when Moses and Paul wrote them. Of all such professors the immutable word of the everlasting God will be found true: "So I sware in My wrath, they shall not enter into My rest." Oh, but who can express the fearfulness of being under such an oath!

The second class of people affected by the immutability of God will be found in the ever gracious word: "All that the Father giveth Me shall come to Me; and him that cometh to Me I will in no wise cast out" (Jno.

vi. 37). And this merciful exercise of immutability has its rise in the divine gift of a certain number of sinners to Christ by His eternal Father. "All that the Father giveth Me." It is united to the priesthood of Christ: "The Lord hath sworn, and will not repent, Thou art a Priest for ever after the order of Melchizedek" (Ps. cx. 4). Here is a mystery, a mercy, and a strong consolation to every sinner who is led to flee for refuge, to lay hold on the hope set before him" (Heb. vi. 18—20). For who shall remove the Lord Jesus from that priesthood in which He was established by the oath of His eternal Father? The oath of exclusion affected the unbelieving rebels only; the oath which made Christ a Priest for ever affects, saves and blesses the whole family of God, the number of which no man can number. By His one offering He perfected for ever them that are sanctified.

In conclusion I exhort you all to keep close to the inspired Word of God. And may He sow in your hearts the incorruptible seed to bring forth fruit, in "some, an hundredfold, in some, sixtyfold, in some, thirtyfold."

Your affectionate friend,

Brighton, February, 1929.   J. K. Popham.

Holy Scripture, etc.

1.

My dear young Friends,—Let me introduce to you a subject of great importance and delight, namely, The Inspiration of the Bible. Its *importance* cannot be exaggerated. It is the fountain of the knowledge of God, of His purposes, love, mercy, wisdom, and power, of heaven and hell. The Bible tells us of creation; of the Fall of Adam and its immediate and everlasting consequences in our corruption, blindness, death, condemnation, and hell, where there is no redemption; regeneration, faith and repentance. It is the instrument of regeneration. In it is the manifestation of Christ

Jesus, the Redeemer, High Priest, Prophet and King. In Holy Scripture God declares His anger with the wicked, and reveals the hell into which impenitent sinners will be cast. In it we see the *necessary* omnipresence of Jehovah in the whole world, and the *gracious*, the *promised* presence of the Trinity in the church. As in a glass we see in the Word of God His sovereign rule in the world, kindly causing His sun to shine on the field of the just and the unjust, not leaving Himself without a witness, and often vindicating His honour by taking vengeance on some of His enemies, making them examples, that others may fear. Oh, what a solemnly important Book do you take in your hands when you take up your Bible to read the customary chapter! May the divine Author open all your eyes that you may behold wondrous things in it; yea, and cause you to feel the tremendous truths it utters as if spoken personally to you.

Then, also, the subject of inspiration is *delightful* in the highest degree. Who is the Author of this Book? By whom did He write it? What are His ends in causing it to be written? Is it infallible? If so, *how?* Each of the above questions is of vast importance, and its investigation will give pleasure to those who are led to consider it. Languages, History, Poetry, Science are delightful to those who take them up as studies. But they have their boundaries; their interest is limited, and also their power to delight. But the *inspiration* of the blessed Word, the revelation of the Almighty, is a *boundless delight.* For its glorious subject—rather should I say, the One Object, the burden of its testimony—is *infinite.*

Turn with me, dear young friends, to the grand subject of INSPIRATION. "This term is used for the mysterious power which the Divine Spirit put forth on the authors of the Scriptures of the Old and New Testament, in order to their composing these as they have been received by the church of God at their hands." This is the definition of divine inspiration L. Gaussen, D.D., gives in his excellent work on "Theopneustia:

the plenary inspiration of the Holy Scriptures." Plenary inspiration gives to the Scriptures their tremendous authority. Such inspiration necessarily excludes the possibility of error. It rendered the inspired writers of the sacred and authoritative Book infallible, though otherwise they were men subject to like passions with ourselves. Thus the Bible *is* the Word of God. The Holy Ghost, in the plenitude of His power, gave the very words of God to the writers of the Scriptures. "Now these be the last words of David. David the son of Jesse said, and the man who was raised up on high, the anointed of the God of Jacob, and the sweet psalmist of Israel, said, *The Spirit of God spake by me, and His word was in my tongue*" (2 Sam. xxiii. 1, 2). This wondrous inspiration is claimed by Peter for the prophets (2 Ep. i. 21). "For the prophecy came not in old time by the will of man, but holy men of God spake as they were moved by the Holy Ghost." "All Scripture" was so inspired—the two Testaments, Old and New. "Every word of God is pure." Without this perfect inspiration that could not be affirmed of "all Scripture." For the fatal flaw of human ignorance would be found in the record. And the crushing sense of fallibility would kill both interest and assurance as we read the Book. Verbal inspiration is that kind of inspiration which imparts not only the matter of the Scriptures, but the exact words by which the matter shall be expressed. The histories, as well as the prophecies, the denunciations, as well as the promises, the gospels, the epistles, the Revelation. The words of the ever adorable Redeemer, and the very words He heard His Father speak, are recorded. The prophecies concerning Him—His Person, Incarnation, sufferings, His shameful death, His piercing cry on the cross, are set before us in the Psalms. Inspiration did not fill the prophets with perfect understanding of all they wrote. They are represented to us as forthreaching after those things which they foretold (1 Pet. i. 10, 11). Their hearts were inflamed with desire to know the mysteries they infallibly uttered, even as doubtless, for the most part, their faith looked to the predicted coming of the Messiah, and rested on the sacrifice of Himself to God for their salvation. They looked forward by faith to the atonement they foretold, as the faith of God's elect to-day looks back, both lookings centred in one spot—Calvary; on one Object—the Lord Jesus.

Do not be carried away by the specious, the deceiving statement that the Bible " contains " the Word of God. Reflect on it. A container is different from what it contains; it holds something which itself is not. We say the Bible IS the Word of God. He gave it. He spoke it. It is infallible. Men will be judged by it. It is the last appeal. It is God's very and immediate Word. By it every man will stand or fall in the last grand assize.

I beg of you all to study this great and deep and mysterious subject. May you be led to do so on your knees, as it were, and with a conviction that you have in your hands the balance of the sanctuary, the golden reed, the measuring line. In the Scripture, Christ is made known as the One whom " every eye shall see," before whom all will be gathered and divided as a shepherd divides his sheep from the goats, to hear their respective everlastingly final words of eternal life and eternal death. Oh that *we* may hear the blessed, the heaven-bestowing words, " Come, ye blessed of My Father, inherit the kingdom prepared for you from the foundation of the world." So desires and prays,

Your affectionate friend,

Brighton, August, 1921. J. K. POPHAM.

2.

My dear young Friends,—My letter to you in last month's *Friendly* was on the great subject of inspiration, a subject worthy of your strict attention. The enemy of souls, and of Immanuel, is doing his utmost to destroy men's natural belief in the sacred revelation, knowing that, in so far as he succeeds, he removes the barrier of the natural reverence and fear of God, and opens the floodgates of profanity, atheism, dishonesty, and all manner of wickedness. When men feel free to cast aside the Bible, there is nothing to rule their consciences, or influence their conduct. Even the Jews, whose great privilege and advantage it was to possess the oracles of God, went into all manner of evil when they cast away their priceless treasure (Rom. iii. 2; Jer. viii. 9). They had the key of knowledge, and took it away from the people. So do our Higher Critics. They wrest from us the Book which God has given us. They tell us that ignorant and prejudiced men wrote it. How can they expect those who believe them to respect the Bible and reverence God and seek to walk according to the Book they themselves have so grievously discredited? Leaving such teachers, the blind leaders of the blind, I will now ask your attention to a point of some consequence in connection with the inspiration of the Word of God, that is, the *necessity* of it.

THE NECESSITY OF INSPIRATION.

1. The necessity of inspiration arises out of our ignorance of the truths of which the Bible treats, and brings to our notice:

(a) Creation. The world is before us, we are in it, part of it. But how, and by whom, it came into being, whence its beauty, the orderly succession of its seasons, the two great lights to rule the day and the night, we know only from the infallible Scriptures: " In the beginning God created the heaven and the earth." " By the word of the Lord were the heavens made, and all the host of them by the breath of His mouth." The planning mind and the working hand may be seen in creation (Gen. i. 1; Ps. xxxiii. 6; Rom. i. 20). Thus even the natural man may perceive God's invisible things in His omnipotent works, while all is beautifully plain to faith (Heb. xi. 3). He left nothing in the work of creation to the uncertain guesses of men. It is infallibly declared to be *His work*. And when atheists and religious infidels ask us to believe that this wonderful world and man, in his physical and immortal being, came of themselves, they ask us to give credit to a

greater miracle than the Holy Scripture reveals, they
invite us to stare at a blank wall before which we are
to stand in the confusion of black and destructive
ignorance and despair; they demand of us that we
insult God, do violence to our conscience, and reject our
chart, our cable—the oracles of God. Blessed for ever
be God that He has given us the only reliable account
of His own work in creation. Following this certain
guide, we shall naturally perceive the beauty of Ps.
cxlviii., where all His works are called on to praise
Him.

(b) The divine Being is not only infinitely above us,
but it is impossible that we should know Him except as
He reveals Himself, and that by those means upon
which we may implicitly rely. Such a revelation He
has been pleased to give, mercifully considering our
ignorance and inability to find Him out. The Bible is
that revelation. By the prophets in old time, by His
Son in these days, He has spoken. His incomprehensible Being, His perfections, must ever have been
unknown and unknowable to creatures if He had not
made them known. But because some have eyes given
them to look on Him and admire Him, He has said in
His Son, "Behold Me" (Heb. i. 1, 2).

He has also revealed His purposes concerning men.
Their positions in providence, their state in eternity, are
from Himself. Everything in them and with respect
to them is from Him; only their sin is excepted in this
their universal dependence. And if it be demanded of
us how we can make such an assertion, the unfaltering
answer is, *the Word of God declares it*. It declares
that "man's goings are of the Lord" (Prov. xx. 24).
Jeremiah knew this well, and confessed, "O Lord, I
know that the way of man is not in himself: it is not
in man that walketh to direct his steps" (x. 23). And
blessedly is this the case with respect to the church (see
Eph. i.; Rom. xi. 11, 15, 16).

(c) Without revelation who can have any knowledge
of a future state ? The conscience of man tells him that
he is accountable to God, and as the judgment does not

take place in this world, there is another world in which he must appear before his Maker and Judge. But a specific knowledge of eternity is not inherent in him. Mercifully, then, revelation, the inspired Bible, comes with its sacred and infallible voice. It informs us of the grand assize, of the books which will then be opened, and of the Book of Life in which are the names of the elect.

(d) Though there is in the natural conscience an idea that God is, and that He must be worshipped, yet, since the Fall, men know not what homage will please Him. Hence the innumerable forms, offerings, prayers and praises which we, in profound ignorance, have evolved out of our own hearts. But, in mercy to His own, the Lord has given forth His mind and will with regard to *how* and with *what* He will be worshipped (Jno. iv. 24; Heb. x. 19—22).

In the above points we may see the necessity of *an inspired Bible*. Think of those points, my friends, and the Lord give you understanding, and a feeling of your own ignorance, and His good Spirit to instruct you. Then you will see the loveliness of an infallible Book, and *feel* its power, and praise its divine Author.

Your affectionate friend,

Brighton, September, 1921.   J. K. POPHAM.

3.

My dear young Friends,—Having called your attention to the tremendously important subject of INSPIRATION, and one of its related subjects, namely, the *necessity* of it, I now ask you to observe the *excellence* of it. This we will call the second of the many related subjects of divine inspiration. In infinite goodness God has made a revelation of Himself and His works. In this blessed revelation there is neither uncertainty nor vagueness.

i. There is no *uncertainty*. "Every word of God is pure." "The words of the Lord are pure words: as silver tried in a furnace of earth, purified seven times."

"All the words of My mouth are in righteousness; there is nothing froward or perverse in them. They are all plain to him that understandeth, and right to them that find knowledge" (Prov. xxx. 5; Ps. xii. 6; Prov. viii. 8, 9). Here, as projected on a mirror, we see the beauteous lines of the absolute certainty of Holy Scripture; it is free from the perplexing defect of that uncertainty which attaches to all things human. When men err, it is because they understand not God in His Word. Christ, whose searching words reach the root of all the matters of which He speaks, told the Sadducees how it was that they denied the resurrection: "Ye do err, not knowing the Scriptures nor the power of God" (Matt. xxii. 29). Though they were acquainted with the Scriptures, they knew them not; neither did they know the power of God subjectively, that is in their hearts, though they saw it objectively, in creation and in the history of their own nation. In this one passage we see that we are taught the inestimable blessing of an infallible Bible. And in passing, let me say how wondrous a mercy it is when the Holy Ghost accompanies the word with His own saving power. For it was not only ignorance of the Scriptures which left the Sadducees to the blind wandering of their own prejudiced hearts, but also their terrible destitution of the power of God. In every revelation they make of God, of His subsistence in a Trinity of Persons, the Eternal Father, the Eternal Son, and the Eternal Spirit: in the histories related, the genealogies recorded, the threatenings thundered, the promises written in blood and confirmed by an oath: in the beatific glimpses of heaven, as the abode of the Bridegroom and His purchased bride, and of the abyss of divine punishment, the dark abode of lost angels and men, given us through the partially-parted veil of Scripture; in all this there is divine certainty. *Every word is true;* and heaven and earth shall pass away, but the word of the living God shall not pass away; all shall be fulfilled. Believing the Scriptures, we believe the "more sure word of prophecy" which "came not in old time by the will of

man; but holy men of God spake as they were moved
by the Holy Ghost" (2 Pet. i. 19, 20).

ii. There is nothing *vague* in the Word of God. All
His words are plain to him that understandeth. To say
there is nothing *vague* in the Scriptures is not saying
there is nothing *mysterious* in them. They contain
many mysterious prophecies, dates, and times, around
which controversies have raged, and which few of the
Lord's people have understood. But whether understood
or not, they are definite in themselves. Mistakes about
them, unnatural, forced meanings attached to them by
men, leave them unaffected. The breath of human
opinion does not sully them. The Eternal Spirit, their
infallible Author, knows His own meaning in them, and
He will, in His own time, bring that to light in acts of
grace in His people, and in solemn, awful providence in
the world. Then will the mouths of false interpreters,
of Arminian teachers, of men who, if possible, would
deceive the very elect, be stopped. Then to each of
them it will be said by Him, " What hast thou to do to
declare My statutes, or that thou shouldest take My
covenant in thy mouth ? " (Ps. l. 16,) While the poor,
weak, fearing people of God, who have been perplexed
about many of their Lord's words and ways, will have
the veil removed from their eyes, their ears shall
hearken, their rash judgments of Him will be corrected,
and they shall say to Him, " Now are we sure that Thou
knowest all things, and needest not that any man should
ask Thee: by this we know that Thou camest forth
from God " (Isa. xxxii. 3, 4; Jno. xvi. 30).

This divine excellence of the Bible will, I hope, be
perceived by you, even naturally. Lacking inspiration,
no superiority of this nature could be claimed for the
Book we revere, but its most necessary character (as the
Word of God) involves the excellence I have claimed
for it. Men blessed with faith *do* rely on it, its every
word they receive, many of them they prove by sweet
experience, they *feel* it to be God's Word to, and in,
their hearts, and to them might, in a spiritual sense, be
addressed the all-comprehensive words of Joshua to

Israel, " And ye know in all your hearts and in all your souls, that not one thing hath failed of all the good things which the Lord your God spake concerning you: all are come to pass unto you, and not one thing hath failed thereof " (Josh. xxiii. 14).

So may you all, dear young readers, come to know the very and immediate Word of God.

Your affectionate friend,

Brighton, October, 1921. J. K. POPHAM.

4.

My dear young Friends,—Once more the vastly important subject of the inspiration of the Word of God is my theme. *The Bible is the Book of books;* it is the only *complete* revelation of God and of His will which we possess. The creation of the world is a revelation of God; some of His invisible things are clearly seen, being understood by the things that are made, even His eternal power and Godhead. Thus all who " deny Him " are without excuse. But this revelation, though beautiful and comprehensive, does not reveal *all* the divine nature; many of the glorious perfections of Deity do not appear in the beneficent consideration of man and beast, which must strike every candid observer of that wondrous work, which its omnipotent Author pronounced " very good."

Providence, too, is a revelation of God. His care of His creatures, of " two sparrows "; His wisdom in guiding all the myriads of human and satanic thoughts, wishes, and intentions of His own designs and ends, turning a designed curse into an undesired blessing, as seen in the selling of Joseph by his jealous brethren, and in Balaam's design to curse Israel (Gen. xxxvii. and xlv. 4—11; Num. xxii. 23). His power in giving to the earth and sea their marvellous reproductiveness to provide for man and beast; His care for the government of nations, giving kings to reign and princes to execute judgment, setting up one and putting down another. All these providences declare the sovereignty, wisdom, and power of Jehovah. Still, notwithstanding, much of His glorious character remains hidden from our eyes, which divine providence was never intended to reveal. For "no man knoweth either love or hatred by all that is before them." No work of God in providence reveals either the one or the other, as standing alone. Yet both love and hatred are in God, in Him as infinite perfections: "Jacob have I loved, but Esau have I hated."

There must then be another revelation of God which discovers Him as *fully* as He chooses to be known. That revelation is the Bible. "All Scripture is given by inspiration of God." Verbal, plenary inspiration alone can give *absolute authority*. God's great end in giving His Word can only be met by such authority. *Consider that end:* For "doctrine, for reproof, for instruction in righteousness: that the man of God may be perfect, throughly furnished unto all good works" (2 Tim. iii. 16, 17).

The authority of the Word of God is inherent. Destroy its authority, and you destroy the Bible. It is proper to it, even as eternity is proper to God. The judgment of the Scriptures is final. There is no appeal from its sentence. All judgment is by a standard; weight is by a balance. The Word answers to both. What *men* say, is right or wrong according to its agreement or disagreement with the Word: "To the law and to the testimony: if they speak not according to this Word, it is because there is no light in them" (Isa. viii. 20). The Scriptures penetrate to the thoughts of man, yea, to every imagination of his thoughts (Gen. vi. 5), and no despising contradiction by any man will invalidate that authoritative statement. The eternal Deity of Christ, His proper Sonship, His vicarious death, His resurrection, His High Priestly work in heaven are all distinctly taught in Holy Scripture, and no man can deny those glorious truths, and be guiltless of trampling underfoot the authority of that sacred Book. In truth, there is no doctrine taught in the Word of God, no conduct commanded, no sin forbidden, no service instituted, no ordinance laid down for observance, no word uttered with respect to God or man, time or eternity, that is not replete with divine authority.

But men acknowledge not this authority. Satan is permitted to blind the minds of them which believe not, lest the light of the glorious gospel of Christ, who is the image of God, should shine unto them. The authority of the Scriptures is abhorrent to the critic. He bows to no authority. His own inner consciousness, aided by his boasted learning, is the only arbiter he will acknowledge. But the light of divine truth will shine in every elect sinner's heart and cause him to tremble at God's Word, causing him to prove the truth of the scripture which says: " The entrance of Thy words giveth light; it giveth understanding unto the simple " (Ps. cxix. 130).

No son or daughter of Adam will escape from the authority of the Word of God. Here or hereafter each one will find that " The Word of God is quick and powerful, and sharper than any two-edged sword, piercing even to the dividing asunder of soul and spirit, and of the joints and marrow, and is a discerner of the thoughts and intents of the heart. Neither is there any creature that is not manifest in His sight: but all things are naked and opened unto the eyes of Him with whom we have to do " (Heb. iv. 12, 13).

May my readers be among those blessed people who have a great High Priest passed into the heavens for them, and so, one day, receive into their hearts the gracious resolve, " Let us therefore come boldly unto the throne of grace, that we may obtain mercy, and find grace to help in time of need."

So prays their affectionate friend,

Brighton, November, 1921.   J. K. POPHAM.

5.

My dear young Friends,—Having addressed to you some observations on the Inspiration of the Bible, I am now going to make a few remarks on the various uses to which the divine Author puts His infallible Book. In all His wondrous works God has an end. Nothing

He has made terminates in itself; all creatures live for an appointed purpose. "For none of us liveth to himself, and no man dieth to himself" (Rom. xiv. 7). The sun and moon were made for a purpose: "And God made two great lights in the firmament of heaven, the greater light to rule the day, and the lesser light to rule the night" (Gen. i. 16). In infinite wisdom, and by omnipotence, God directs and works all things to their predestined end—His glory. "For of Him, and through Him, and to Him are all things: to whom be glory for ever. Amen" (Rom. xi. 36; Prov. xvi. 4).

Now the truth of a divinely predestinated use and end for all things applies in an eminent degree to the verbally, plenarily inspired Scriptures. Emphatically it has its appointed uses. All I can attempt in monthly letters is to just point out, in a general way, the great matters I am anxious you should know.

The uses to which the glorious Inspirer of the Scriptures puts them are, (i.) *To give to the church a knowledge of God:* "God, who at sundry times and in divers manners spake in time past unto the fathers by the prophets, hath in these last days spoken unto us by His Son" (Heb. i. 1, 2). The blessedness of man, as created in Adam, consisted in the knowledge of God. The trees of the garden were the bountiful gift of the Creator, and spoke to Adam of Him, but there was then a knowledge only of good. The forbidden tree would (if, and when, eaten of) give knowledge of evil as contrasted with good; would bring the knowledge of disobedience, of shame, of terror, and of displeasure in the law-Giver. From that eventful day man has lived in ignorance of, and enmity to, God. And for this ignorance and enmity there is no remedy but the one which God Himself found and provided: His election of Christ to be the Saviour of the church, which is His body. To Adam and Eve this remedy was preached and brought; to Abel the gospel of sacrifice was taught, while Cain was left in ignorance and enmity. From that day till Christ came in the flesh the Lord manifested Himself to individual persons, then to the nation He chose and "separated from all the people that are upon the face of the earth." To that chosen nation the Lord made Himself known by prophets, types and shadows, and by such means gave the form of worship wherein He was duly honoured. But when Christ came, the adumbration gave place to a distinct manifestation. "And" now, "without controversy great is the mystery of godliness: God was manifested (margin) in the flesh" (1 Tim. iii. 16). This glorious manifestation of God was, and is, in the church (ver. 15). And every child of God, according to divine ordination, is taught of the Father this great and glorious mystery, and so comes to Christ (John vi. 45). (ii.) The next use the Most High God makes of the Scriptures is *to beget His people.* "Of His own will begat He us with the word of truth, that we should be a kind of firstfruits of His creatures" (Jas. i. 18). Who can number the people to whom a threatening word out of the law, or a scripture concerning God, or eternity, heaven or hell, was made spirit and life, imparting to them a new nature? This is an exceedingly solemn and blessed use which the Spirit makes of the inspired Word. (iii.) The next use which is made of the Word is *to give light.* "The entrance of Thy Word giveth light: it giveth understanding to the simple" (Ps. cxix. 130). Here is the instruction of wisdom, justice, judgment and equity. The knowledge of God and His claims on a sinner; of His holy law, and its inability to give life to one dead in trespasses and sins; of Christ and His work of redemption; of the Holy Ghost and His office in the church as the Spirit of wisdom and revelation in the knowledge of Christ, and of His cleansing blood, His justifying righteousness. (iv.) The fourth use of Holy Scripture is *to admonish, warn and exhort the saints,* to set before them their duties, as now brought into a new relationship to God. (v.) *In the open, public preaching, the Scriptures are used to warn the wicked,* to tell them of their sad, lost, dead and guilty condition, and that, dying in that condition, they must endure the wrath of God for ever. (vi.) *The Word informs us of the coming*

D

day of judgment, when all the nations of the earth shall
be gathered before God, the Judge of all (Matt. xxv.
31—46). (vii.) Yet another and important use the
Spirit will have His own Word put to is, that Christ's
commission to His apostles first, and then to every sent
minister to the end of the world, shall be fulfilled: " Go
ye into all the world, and preach the gospel to every
creature " (Mark xvi. 15, 16; Matt. xxviii. 18—20).
This is for the gathering to " one fold " all the blood-
bought sheep.

The above are some of the uses which the Spirit
makes of holy Scripture. They are wonderful uses, of
vast importance, and issue in the glory of God " in the
church by Christ Jesus throughout all ages, world
without end. Amen " (Eph. iii. 21).

Of course, you will have observed that in my letter to
you on Inspiration and its uses, I have assumed that
you do believe in the wondrous work of the Holy Ghost
in His chosen penmen. I have deliberately used simple
language; all technical terms have been avoided, except
those most commonly used when inspiration is con-
tended for, viz., verbal and plenary, the meaning of
which you all know.

When you read these lines, the last month of the year
will have come. To many the year will have seemed
astonishingly short, and the few remaining days of it,
added to those which have fled, may remind us that
" we spend our years as a tale that is told," and that
soon *we* must " pass the gloomy vale." O, but if we
have given to us eternal life, if the Lord has spoken
peace by the blood of Christ, if we know Christ by the
revelation of Him in us, if we have received the sealing
of the Spirit, *all is well.*

With every good wish for your temporal and eternal
welfare,

    I am, my dear young friends,

        Your affectionate friend,

Brighton, December, 1921.   J. K. POPHAM.

6.

Consequences of denying Inspiration.

My dear young Friends,—I concluded my last letter to you by advising you to meet all critics of the Bible with one word, " Inspiration." What is meant by " All Scripture is given by inspiration of God," the critics do not agree among themselves. Some deny and reject all miraculous inspiration, attributing to it no more than they do to poets. Others, while admitting a divine inspiration, restrict it to a part only of the Word of God. There is yet a third class of critics, who extend inspiration to all parts of the Bible, but not *equally* to all. Thus men, denying God, some entirely, others partly, in His Word, become lost in uncertainties. We will leave them in the mists of their own guesses, and attend to the ever-blessed, plenary, verbal inspiration of the Scriptures of which we are assured by the apostle Paul, " all Scripture is God-breathed." The apostle Peter tells us: " Holy men of old spake as they were moved by the Holy Ghost " (2 Pet. i. 21). And Peter elucidates the words of " the sweet Psalmist of Israel who said, The Spirit of the Lord spake by me, and His word was in my tongue " (2 Sam. xxiii. 2), and of all the writers of the Old Testament from Moses to Malachi.

I want you to consider with me one or two terrible consequences of the denial of the inspiration of the Bible. i. *The rejection of the beautiful, awe-inspiring account of Creation:* " In the beginning God created the heaven and the earth." Did the Eternity, the Majesty, the Omnipotence, the glory of " I AM THAT I AM " ever appear to any of you as you read that account ? And did you recollect at the same time that it was the Word who was with God, and who was God, who made the things that Moses tells us were made by God ? (Gen. i.; Jno. i. 1—3; Heb. i. 2.) But none of these things can be rightly believed unless we have faith (Heb. xi. 3). Now ask yourselves: " What is it that gives men, learned men, liberty to believe and teach Evolution ?

The answer is, "The utter rejection of Inspiration." Men who reject that mysterious truth may easily, in their judicial blindness, sing of the *poetry* of Gen. i., and repudiate those parts of the books of Moses which they think to be mistakes, or of later dates.

ii. *Think of the bewildering uncertainty, which the denial of Inspiration throws us into.* It leads to nowhere in this life. Put an uncertain, that is, an uninspired Bible into my hand; tell me that *that* book will teach me the way to flee from the wrath to come, which, knowing that I deserve it, I am fearing. But I say, "How am I to know that it is to be depended on?" The critic answers, "Oh, *we* know which parts were given by Inspiration and which were not." Again I ask, nay, I demand, for my case is urgent, "*How do you know?*" He replies: "By my learning, my researches, and my inner consciousness." Here I object, "You ask me to place my confidence, my trust, in you, a man like myself, in your learning which is successfully opposed by learning greater than yours, by researches far beyond yours, which prove to a demonstration that your data are false, unfounded. How can I trust an uncertain guide, a fallible man, when my search is for a city which hath foundations, whose Builder and Maker is God?" "Inner consciousness"! What is that? A conclusion which an unbeliever in God, a man whose carnal mind is enmity against God, arrives at; a foregone conclusion that, as God is not truly in all his thoughts, so neither is that divine Being in Creation, in the history of the Bible, in the virgin birth, in the vicarious atonement of the Incarnate Son, in His resurrection. All is mist, miasma, poison, eternal death, on the ground of the rejection, in whole or in part—the "in part" being worse, if possible, than utter rejection —of the divine, therefore infallible, Inspiration of the Holy Scriptures.

Oh, my friends, beware of this terrible heresy of no— or part—Inspiration. By it you have no ground. There is no uncertainty in the Scripture teaching respecting God, God in Christ, the Father, the Son, and the Holy

Ghost; respecting sin, condemnation, and salvation for all for whom the Lord Jesus, the Son of God Incarnate, died. The Lord help you to believe, hold fast, and love *an Inspired Bible*, and grant to you to be begotten with the Word of truth, that you may know that " with Him there is no variableness, neither shadow of turning " (James i. 17—21).

Your affectionate friend,

Brighton, February, 1926. J. K. POPHAM.

7.

Advantages of belief in Inspiration.

My dear young Friends,—In my last letter I spoke of the sin, and some consequences, of *the rejection* of the inspired Word of God. May I hope that you seriously considered the important matter ? That you see the evil of rejecting the Word which He has magnified above all His Name ? That you see it is a wicked thing to adversely judge that Book which will judge all men ? This month I wish you to consider with me *the advantage* of believing the verbal inspiration of the " Scripture which cannot be broken." The advantage may be seen in the following particulars:—

i. When the believer in the inspiration of it takes up the Bible to read, there is a sense of certainty; he believes that every word of God is pure, and free from error. This is an immense advantage. The chief advantage of the Jews was that " unto them were committed the oracles of God " (Rom. iii. 1, 2). And though some did not believe, God who gave that covenant nation His Word, is faithful and He will fulfil it; and as it is " the word of truth," by it He begets His people that they may be a kind of firstfruits. Heaven and earth shall pass away before one word of God shall miss fulfilment. All that Holy Scripture reveals of God, of His purposes, love, justice, wisdom and power; all that He says of men, good and evil, and their ultimate destinations, shall be made good, and be fully manifested throughout eternity. The histories, prophecies, promises, threatenings were verbally inspired, and will live in the truth and fulfilment of them throughout eternity. Certainty in natural things is necessary for comfort, how much more in things eternal. Remember then this first fruit, and contrast it with the blank, dismal, disconcerting, oscillating, sinful, dangerous condition of those men who deny, either in whole or in part, the perfect inspiration of the Scriptures.

ii. Our apprehensions of God and His ways can only be right as we receive the revelation of Himself and of them from His Word. I speak not here of the work of the Holy Ghost in the regenerate, but of our natural and rational perception of what the Bible says. I speak reverently of God, the true and living God, but a strange being is he of whom the Evolutionist, the Socinian, and the Arminian speak and write. He did not create the world over which he is supposed to rule, for it came somehow into being of itself; he cannot be a Trinity, for such a thing as three in one and one in three is against, contrary to reason; he cannot be happy, because he is ever anxious to save men and make them happy; he cannot succeed, because men refuse his offers and thwart his efforts. O what folly, what wickedness, what blindness and madness seize and control men when they deny God in His Word! Dear young people, follow, read, with diligence, the Word of God, and the Lord give you understanding that you may live.

iii. The gospel, an integral part of the Bible, a large part of it, is a glorious light (2 Cor. iv. 4). It is impossible to express the wickedness of the contemners of it, as all are who deny verbal inspiration. But it will ever be the glorious gospel; and to the people who sit in darkness, and in the region and shadow of death, this light springs up (Matt. iv. 15, 16). The sacrifice of the Lord Jesus was, and will everlastingly be, vicarious; and therefore His blood will ever be sufficient for the free and full pardon of all those who, by the Spirit's grace, confess and forsake their sins. Whatever mist of ignorance, whatever bar of unbelief, there may be in our hearts, the light of the glorious gospel is sufficient to remove. The light of the gospel reveals God in His gracious nature, in His justice and love, for both justice and love are in His gift of His only begotten Son; it reveals Him in His benign intentions to sinners, His faithfulness to His promises which in Christ are yea and amen; in the ultimate end of His people both as to their souls and bodies; at death they join the spirits of just men made perfect, and harp with the harpers, and sing as it were a new song before the throne; and in the resurrection their bodies will be fashioned like unto the glorious body of the Lord Jesus (Rev. xiv. 2, 3; Phil. iii. 21; 1 Jno. iii. 1, 2). The Word of God states all the above. There is nothing cloudy, misty, uncertain, or contradictory, all is infallible, all from the lip of divine truth, from the faithful and true Witness.

The same clear, unequivocal testimony is given with regard to the world which lieth in wickedness. Men say in their hearts and in their lives they will not have the God-Man to reign over them, but rebellion does not render the Sovereign impotent. He is long-suffering, but He is terrible in His justice. Besides the " Book of Life," in which are the names of " the redeemed from among men," there are other books, and the lost will be " judged out of those things which were written " therein. All eternally sure, spoken by God that cannot lie. May He give us faith to receive and hold fast to the inerrant Book which He has mercifully given to man, and by means of which He begets His own children, and declares Himself to be the God of salvation.

iv. There is a blessed prospect before the people of God. A divine vista is opened in the Scriptures, " spirits of just men made perfect, harpers with their harps, crowned with a crown of life;" and also with respect to their bodies the infallible Word sets forth an everlasting future of shining glory, for Christ " shall change our vile body, that it may be fashioned like unto His glorious body, according to the working whereby He is able even to subdue all things unto Himself " (Phil. iii. 21; also 1 Jno. iii. 1, 2).

Deny inspiration, and all I have said is uncertain. God give each one to hold fast the divine inspiration of the Bible. Jesus Christ is the faithful and true Witness, and what He said of saints and the ungodly is true, everlastingly true. May the Holy Ghost give us faith in Him and His holy Word.

Your affectionate friend,

Brighton, April, 1926.   J. K. POPHAM.

8.

My dear young Friends,—Though I am writing only a letter, I will have for a foundation a text out of God's Word. My text is: " Thy Word is a lamp unto my feet, and a light unto my path " (Ps. cxix. 105). To the Psalmist " Thy Word " was all that was then written of Holy Scripture, the law of commandments, and the ceremonial law, which was a shadow of good things to come, and which was sufficient to make him wise unto salvation, and enable him to walk according to the revealed will of God. We know, by his life and Psalms, that the word of Christ dwelt in him richly in all wisdom. To the church of God to-day " Thy Word " means the whole of the infallible Word, as she possesses it. The two Testaments, Old and New, " came not in old time by the will of man, but holy men of God spake as they were moved by the Holy Ghost " (2 Pet. i. 21).

Now a very clear inference to be drawn from my text is, that all who walk without God's Word, walk in darkness, and know not at what they stumble. " The way of the wicked is as darkness; they know not at what they stumble;" " If any man walk in the day, he stumbleth not, because he seeth the light of this world. But if a man walk in the night, he stumbleth, because there is no light in him " (Prov. iv. 19; Jno. xi. 9, 10). Consider this. When people go to the theatre, the cinema, or to balls, and to dances, and the many things which always accompany such amusements, they are walking in darkness, that is, without the Word of God, and the illumination of the Holy Ghost in that Word in their hearts. And when religious people are occupied with the social side of religion, their pleasant meetings where each is pleased to see his friend, and there is no gospel, no grace in spirit or speech, is not this walking in a vain show? Yet they appear to be beguiled into a belief that all is well; a religious lullaby is sung, and sleeping and slumbering in a carnal security is the result. The Word of God is the only true, infallible guide. What is required of us as God's creatures, both to Himself and our neighbours, the Word informs us. To enable us to see this our double duty the Bible is given to us. It is a lamp to our feet, and a light to our path. And it is necessary that we should have the teaching of the Spirit if ever we are to see what is right. Our feet do not guide us when we walk; the whole body is opaque except the eye. That wonderful organ receives light, imprints images of things on the brain, and so we see what to avoid, and where we may walk with safety. Thus to the heart and understanding the Word comes by its divine Author's inshining, and is the true light. But even naturally the Word of God is a light to all who read it in simplicity and without the false and bewildering flicker of the unbelieving Critic. Turn, then, with God's Word, to Genesis i. and ii. There Moses gives the account of our origin. I often read these chapters and I believe them to be the divinely given history of our beginning, of our relation to God, and of our receiving the law written in our hearts, Rom. ii. 14, 15. From this law we cannot absolve ourselves. The Critic will find himself bound in the chains of a perfect law, unless redeemed by Christ, as indeed we all shall, if not partakers of the same redemption.

I want to show you the supreme and everlasting importance of the creation of Adam by God. On the divine accuracy of that work of omnipotence hang the verity of the Scriptures, and two foundation doctrines. If God did not create man in His own image, then the Word of God is not true, it deceives us in saying He did. I put the statement in this form that you may see the awful consequences of denying any statement of the "Scripture of truth." Every person who denies the creation of Adam by the wise omnipotence of God, makes God a liar. For He declares by Moses that He did create and make him. Make but one Scripture untrue and you make the whole Bible unreliable. But "every word is pure," that is, *absolutely true.* My dear young friends, *hold fast Genesis i. and ii.,* that is, hold fast the whole of the Word of God as verbally, plenarily inspired.

A fundamental doctrine hangs on the creation of Adam by God, as related in Genesis i. and ii. Adam's Headship of the whole of the human race. No promiscuous man, coming nobody knows how or when, emerging from something, nobody knows what, could be the proper Head of the human family. See the confusion in which the denial of God's Word at once involves men. But the Lord made Adam the Head of his family. And the first indication of this is in the marriage union. "And Adam said, This is now bone of my bones, and flesh of my flesh. . . . Therefore shall a man leave his father and his mother, and shall cleave unto his wife: and they shall be one flesh" (Gen. ii. 23, 24; Matt. xix. 5; Mark x. 6—10). And that law is in force to-day. In regard to the human race there is one Head. "The first man Adam was made a living soul," and he conveys his natural and moral life and character to his posterity. Thus in a twofold sense Adam was made a living soul. If this were not so, how can Rom. v. 12 and 1 Cor. xv. 22 be explained and made just and righteous? The doctrine of representation is a fundamental doctrine of the Scripture, and I bring it before you because the integrity of the Scripture is bound up with it. The Headship of the Lord Jesus is linked with that of Adam, linked as type and Antitype. Destroy the type and how will you retain the Antitype? Adam was made a living soul to convey his nature to all his family. This is the type. Now see the wonderful Antitype: ". . . the last Adam was made a quickening Spirit;" and "as is the heavenly, such are they also that are heavenly." As these two Heads are thus given us, and joined by the Holy Ghost in Holy Scripture,

you cannot destroy the first and leave the second un-
touched. But how can we walk in the path of such
mysteries? Only by the lamp and the light. Oh then
what a mercy it is to have an infallible Bible! Leave
the wicked men (who, with their axes and hammers of
so-called learning, cut down the carved work of the
blessed Word of God), and follow that Word. Remember that "Evil communications corrupt good manners;"
you cannot step on burning coal and not be burned, you
cannot take pitch into your hand and not be blackened.

May God be gracious to you, and cause you to know
and *feel* the importance, yea, the vital necessity of His
Word, and give it to you, even as He gave it to His
disciples (Jno. xvii. 8).

Your affectionate friend,

Brighton, March, 1927. J. K. POPHAM.

9.

*An Address delivered at the Trinitarian Bible Society's
Meeting, held in Brighton, October 3rd, 1929.*

The account of Creation in grandly simple language;
the generations of men and the formation of families;
the flood and the miraculous preservation of the human
race; the history of nations in the world's infancy; the
divine call of Abraham, and God's covenant with him,
and its renewal with Isaac and Jacob; the sojourn and
oppression of Israel in Egypt, and her deliverance; the
history of the wondrous theocracy; the captivity of the
covenant people for their sins; the preservation of the
kingly tribe of Judah, who ruled with God till Christ
came; the record of the virgin birth; the Saviour's
substitutionary life, given in touching simplicity; the
account of His vicarious death, told in awful dignity
and majesty; His resurrection and ascension into heaven;
the day of Pentecost, and the subsequent and consequent
ministry of the everlasting gospel, and its glorious success; Christ's care of the newly-planted churches, ex-
hibited in the Epistles; the descriptive and prophetic
Book of Revelation,—all these matters constitute the

Bible, and were given by inspiration. The inspiration of the Scripture sets it alone, above, and different from every other book that has existed, does exist, and shall exist. The Bible is what it is because it is the inspired Word of God. It is therefore absolutely unique. We call it the " Holy Bible "; it is supremely, exclusively so. It is holy in the sense of being written by inspiration, and infallible. It is not composed of words chosen by the human writers of it to express thoughts which the Holy Ghost suggested; they spake as they were *moved* [inspired] by the Holy Ghost. They constantly say the word of the Lord came to them, the Spirit of God spake to and by them. Inerrancy requires that God should choose His own words. The revelation of Himself, of His will and purposes, must needs be made to man in His own pure words. The man of business will dictate his own words to his secretary in all his business letters; he will not trust that his secretary will correctly express important, delicate, and complicated matters, which might be given to him in general terms. Much less would the Holy Ghost say to His penmen, "Write to the *effect*." No, the deep things of God must be expressed by Himself. The words must be His own. He must say His own things in His own words. His things are eternal. They are the Being of God, His eternity, His perfections, His subsistence in three Persons, bearing the essential names of Father, Son, and Holy Ghost, showing their distinct Personalities, their eternal equality. Only God could, in the first place, utter the sublime sentence, " In the beginning was the Word, and the Word was with God, and the Word was God," it is too profoundly incomprehensible and glorious for merely human expression (Jno. i. 1). And again, verses 14 and 18: " And the Word was made flesh, and dwelt among us, (and we beheld His glory, the glory as of the only-begotten of the Father,) full of grace and truth. . . . No man hath seen God at any time; the only-begotten Son, which is in the bosom of the Father, He hath declared Him." A mere suggestion of such divine truths would have shattered the mind which was required to express it in correct and adequate terms, by its very weight, mystery, and glory. Only an involuntary pen, under the absolute control of the divine Dictator, could write such awfully grand and blessed words. Thus the Bible makes revelations of the eternal, internal acts of Jehovah, and who but Himself knew how to put those mysteries into human language?

This divine Book states most explicitly the Fall of man. It tells us that man was made upright, and under the law to God, His Creator. Here we must find man's responsibility to God, a better word perhaps is *account-ability*, accountability of which we cannot divest ourselves. The Bible reveals the second Man, the last Adam, who is a quickening Spirit to His seed.

It must not be omitted to state that a holy and wise providence has a prominent, honourable, important place in our inerrant Bible; it is, as it were, the handmaid of grace. The lives of some individual persons, the histories of some nations, are related. Its accuracy in these is matchless; its impartiality inimitable. Viewed from every standpoint it may be confidently affirmed that no merely human mind or hand could have produced our infallible Bible. *It is the very and immediate Word of the Holy Ghost.* The penmen were His instruments. The holy, beautiful words of revelation, of description, of history, of promise, of threat, were traced on the original parchments as He dictated them. Both the Testaments, Old and New, thus bear the ineffaceable stamp of divine origin, that is, of verbal, plenary inspiration. Moreover, by His numerous quotations from the Old Testament, the Lord Jesus Christ has welded it into the New Testament, and thus they are manifestly one organic whole. They have but one voice. They stand or fall together. " The testimony of Jesus is the spirit of prophecy " (Rev. xix. 10). The sanction of the adorable Trinity is on Holy Scripture.

I judge we are now in a position to adopt and lay down the proposition with which Dr. Owen opens his work on the divine original of the Scripture, viz.: " That the whole authority of the Scripture in itself, depends solely on its divine original, is confessed by all who acknowledge its authority." I hold that that proposition is absolutely correct. The Word of God can receive no accession of authority from any human source. It is a perfect Word. And it is indefectible. It is the sole and everlasting rule of faith and practice. Against this divine rule both the Papist and the Modernist object. The former, that he may introduce and place above Holy Scripture his necessary tradition; the latter, that he may honour his own intellect and inner consciousness— whatever that may be. Alas, divine authority is abhorrent to fallen man. The Papist has numberless idols, the Modernist has but one. He must rid himself of the incubus of Authority, otherwise he must bow down to the Bible. Rejecting that, as to its full, complete inspiration, he thinks himself at liberty to edit it, correct it, criticise its facts, question its doctrines, shorten it, omitting what he objects to, and to tell us what God ought to be, what He cannot do, and what He is ever attempting to do, but is unable to accomplish. Be it given to us to bow before Jehovah and reverence His Word, which He has exalted above all His Name.

November, 1929.

10.

My dear young Friends,—The Bible is the foundation of all certain knowledge of God, the infallible guide through the intricacies of life, the only reliable testimony of Jesus, and the final appeal of all controversies. Therefore, the first aim and effort of the Modernist is to destroy belief in its inerrancy. It must then be our aim to keep close to it as given by inspiration of God. If we be cut away from this, all is lost, and what then shall we do? However, puny man can really do nothing against this wonderful Rock. The Psalmist tells the most blessed truth when he says, "For ever, O Lord, Thy Word is settled in heaven" (Ps. cxix. 89). That solemn word was inspired concerning those books of Holy Scripture that were then written, and without violence or stretching it must be said of all the Books which now comprise the sacred Volume. To compose the blessed revelation of Himself, and His purposes and His works, it pleased the Lord to occupy many generations. He used holy men of old as His amanuenses. One has said, " I fear not to say they were His pens." A most true word. And what they wrote were the words of God. If they wrote what is called "profane history," they wrote facts at His dictation. And when they were to write of Jehovah, and His love to a fallen church, and His purposes concerning the human race, time, eternity, heaven, hell, and the kind of persons who should dwell in them, how could they write of such out of their own minds? If only suggestions of matters of eternal importance were made to them, can we imagine the holy penmen capable of finding suitable, infallibly accurate terms or words to express and convey to their countless readers the fulness of the suggestions? A human mind able to express Jehovah! He puts no confidence in His saints. He is gloriously wise. He knew how to convey the truth concerning Himself to men. Even when the disciples of Christ should be taken unto the synagogues, and unto magistrates and powers, they were to take no thought how or what things they should answer or say. "For the Holy Ghost shall teach you in the same hour what ye ought to say " (Luke xii. 11, 12). So jealous is God of His Word. So important is the testimony of Christ. So likewise, God, alone knowing His own counsel and will and purpose, gives the words that express them infallibly. The words of the law were written by the finger of God. His word came to Abraham, Isaac, and Jacob, to Moses, to Samuel, to the sweet Psalmist of Israel, to Isaiah, to Jeremiah, and to all the prophets, to the four writers of the gospels, to the apostles who penned the epistles. The Modernist calls this perfect inspiration, mechanical. The answer to this groundless objection is that each writer retained his own personality which the Holy Ghost so used as to make what he spoke or wrote the very Word of God.

Let us, therefore, hold fast by the inspired, infallible Word.

Many scholars, colleges, and ministers of religion, so called, are against the pure Word of God. Recently at " an exceptionally large attendance in Congregation " it was " proposed to abolish the Examination in Holy Scripture. . . . Mr. Parker, of Magdalen, who sponsored the promulgation of the statute, said that it had been brought forward at the request of more than 130 members of the Congregation. Honours schools, he added, had been making increased demands on the time and attention of those reading for them, and yet the University compelled its members to forego a considerable amount of the time which should be devoted to their special studies to prepare themselves for an examination in the rudiments of Holy Scripture. . . . The preamble to the statute was passed by 150 votes to 91." Thus the ancient University of Oxford has, in an important sense, rejected the inspired Book, while its students are led to believe that it is more important to take " honours " than to know the Word of God. So does Modernism prevail. May God, in His mercy, preserve you, my young friends, from the denial of the inspiration of Holy Scripture, and specially give you the best proof of its inerrancy by *feeling* the power of it in your own souls.

Your affectionate friend,

Brighton, February, 1932.   J. K. POPHAM.

11.

An Address delivered at the Annual Meeting of the Trinitarian Bible Society (Brighton Branch), on Thursday Evening, October 20th, 1932.

I suppose that all of us believe in the inspiration, verbal inspiration, of Holy Scripture, rendering it inerrant, infallible, that its every word is inspired, that wicked deeds related here were related by direct inspiration of the Holy Ghost. Taking this for granted, one has no need to make any further observation on that most important point.

i. I would like just to make one or two observations about the power of Holy Scripture. There is power when the Spirit of Christ, who inspired the Scripture, takes of it and applies it to any purpose, in either a person or a church. To a child of God, or in regard to a reprobate, there is power. It can never be turned aside. It always goes straight to that point to which it is directed. Clothed in His light, and armed with His own power, the Scripture goes to its ordained point or object. " He sent out His Word," we read. What for ? To heal the sick people to whom He sent it. " He sent His Word and healed them," and they were healed, it could not fail of its purpose.

Now the power of the Word is expressed thus: " Is not My word like a fire ? " This expresses force: the fire consumes. It is sent to consume the self-righteousness of a redeemed person, and fire produces ashes, and the ashes fit the person for the beauty of Christ, for He is sent to " give beauty for ashes." Self-righteous people resist as far as they can. That is to say, when one is brought under the teaching of the Spirit, and God will consume his self-righteousness, he goes about as much as he possibly can to establish his own righteousness; but the fire does its appointed work. One word comes; and if that seems insufficient, another comes, and yet another. As one has expressed it in other terms: " If one blow is not sufficient, God deals another." If He will reduce you, if He will reduce me, to that state by the Spirit of burning and of judgment, we shall come into the ashes.

ii. The Scripture is likened also to a hammer: " Is not My Word like a hammer, to break the rock in pieces ? " Men have stony, rocky hearts, and would, if possible, resist Jehovah. " But who hath resisted His will ? " Those of us to whom the Word has been made a hammer have reason, yea, everlasting reason, to thank God that He would not be put off, or turned aside from His work, by our ignorant cries. It is great to be under the power of God's Word, so that what is in opposition to His will is broken down. Proud reason is broken, and the man comes into that Scripture: " If any man will be wise in this world, let him become a fool, that he may be wise." Proud, haughty spirits come down under the power of the Word of God, and wild affections are restrained, and gathered up by the power of God's holy Word.

iii. The Scripture is also used to sanctify. Christ's prayer, you will remember, is, " Sanctify them through Thy truth; Thy Word is truth." This sanctification is different from that vamped-up holiness men boast of. When the word comes—the word of grace, of life, of mercy, of peace, of truth, it has such an effect on the heart as to gather and set apart for God the favoured person in his affections, his will, his judgment, his desires, his designs. He is sanctified. As you know, the word signifies, " to set apart," to set apart from a common to a particular use. Wherever God graciously goes to a sinner (He came to call sinners to repentance), then He sets up that great work of sanctification. Not the bettering of fallen nature, but the setting apart of the sinful person for His own glory.

iv. Also the Scripture is for nourishment. Jeremiah said, " Thy words were found, and I did eat them; and Thy word was unto me the joy and rejoicing of my heart." Well, that is wonderful. That teaches a man that he " does not live by bread alone, but by every word that proceedeth out of the mouth of the Lord doth man live." It is a great thing to have this Word that will nourish you in any circumstances. You come into a trouble that scatters you, or self-will comes, or a spirit of rejection of the cross. You say you cannot bear it, and perhaps you say you won't bear it. But God says, " You shall." And how does He do it ? He takes of His word, and by His good Spirit drops it into the heart, and the sinner, instead of saying, " I won't," says, " Lord, may I be enabled to take it up ? " Instead of saying, " I cannot bear it," he says, " I can do all things through Christ that strengtheneth me." The Word nourishes faith: "Nourished up in the words of faith and good doctrine."

v. It is also joy and rejoicing: "Thy words were found, and I did eat them; and Thy word was unto me the joy and rejoicing of my heart." If God tells you that He loves you, that will be joy to you. If He tells you that some affliction that is on you is sent, not in anger, but in His love, His covenant love, that will be joy and rejoicing. Why, you will lose your trouble, even though you have to carry it, for the joy of the Lord is your strength.

vi. The Scripture is also a lamp, a lamp to the feet to guide, to tell you which way to go, to open to your view dangers which, by that view of them, you may escape. It is good to have the Word of God to guide you.

Well, in these things Holy Scripture is just *the* Book, and if by means of the Trinitarian Bible Society, one copy of the Scriptures falls into the hand of a redeemed person, no matter where, it accomplishes a wonderful purpose and is worthy of support. Let us remember what the Word of God is. It is His own Word. I like the word "verbal." To make the Scripture the Word of God and infallible, it must be a verbal inspiration. Think of it! An employer has a secretary. Some unimportant letter has to be answered, and the master says, "Say so-and-so," and gives him a correct form, but leaves the particular words to the secretary. He has an important matter to deal with. The secretary sits at his side, and the master dictates every word; so though the hand that wrote the letter was the hand of the secretary, the words were the words of the master. God chose instruments, inspired writers; but as Jeremiah, as Ezekiel, and as the prophets said generally, "The word of the Lord came to me," "The word of the Lord came expressly to me," not thoughts for me to express as I might choose, not doctrines which I might put in my own form, but words, the very words of the living God. We should treasure this Book. The Modernist takes it out of our hand.

" Ah," he says, " some parts of it are inspired." I say
to him, " Will you assure me what parts are inspired ?
How can you ? If only a part of this verse is inspired,
will you tell me how you know that the other part is
not ? If some part of the Holy Word is not inspired,
how am I to know that any part is ? " We must receive
the Word as the whole Word, or not at all. If I believed
what the Modernist says, I should throw my Bible away.
I should have no use for it. To whom do you think
God will allocate the guilt of very much of the sabbath-
breaking to-day ? I believe God will allocate much of
the guilt of sabbath-breaking to the teaching of the
Modernist in the pulpit, for he is doing his utmost to
destroy in the minds of the people respect for the
Scriptures. If he makes me believe that the whole
Bible is not inspired, but only some parts of it, why
should I respect any part of it ? Sin comes by the law.
That is to say, " Where no law is, there is no transgression." And if the sabbath, the Lord's day that we
have, is not of divine institution, why should we observe
it ? You may see how the Scripture thus dealt with will
bring you to disrespect and disregard the Word of God.
By this men are to be judged, by this they are to be
justified, by this they are to be condemned, by this they
will reach heaven or be consigned to hell.

The Trinitarian Bible Society is worthy of support
because it contends for, and circulates the inspired Word
of God without any of the insertions of the Douay
Bible. It is our Authorised Bible which this Society
circulates, and it is good for us to support it to the
utmost of our ability. It may be said, " Oh, but a little
of the Romish teaching won't hurt us." You fill this
tumbler with pure water, and then put a few drops of
arsenic in it, will you drink it ? Death is in it. The
Lord help us to hold fast by the inspired Scripture, and
to circulate, as well as we can, this blessed Book.

December, 1932.

Conduct, Morals, General Advice, etc.

1.

My dear Readers,—This month's letter to you shall be on the very important subject of reading. Of course, you are readers. Everybody reads to-day. Alas! the *kind* of reading is, for the most part, unwholesome; and the effect, evil. I take it, however, that all, or nearly all, who care to take up the *Friendly Companion,* have an example worthy of imitation in this particular matter of reading. You may have been accustomed to a chapter of the Bible in the morning, and another in the evening, followed by prayer. May the influence of that good example be lasting, leading you to read the sacred page for yourselves. There is no other book to be compared with it; it alone is infallible, it alone, therefore, can be implicitly believed, for it contains no error. It is the very Word of God; a revelation of the divine Majesty. And should the Holy Ghost, who inspired holy men of old to write it, *apply* any part of it to your conscience, you would at once know, though you might not immediately understand, the power of God in it. After the Bible come other books. And here I urge upon you the need of care in your *selection.* Much, very much of the literature of the day is unsafe. Against *two* kinds allow me to warn you. i. *General religious literature.* ii. *Novels.* EXCLUDE THEM BOTH. You must, you ought to read. "Reading," it has been well said, "makes a full man." Cultivate the habit of reading while you are young. Later in life you may find less leisure for so delightful an occupation and recreation. Read history, read Church history. If you read it attentively you will see how wonderfully God has taken care of His honour, and supported and comforted His people in their afflictions and persecutions. You will find much of this manifestation of God in Milner's "Church History," and you would quickly find the work deeply interesting. D'Aubigné's "History of the Reformation" would fascinate you. His motto would grip you, "God in History." Then, master Wylie's "History of Protestantism." You would there see, as in a glass, what Popery is, and what she has done to God's people. You would find much to interest you in the "Antiquities of the Jews," by Flavius Josephus.

I would next recommend Biographies. What a field is here! There are many other good books which I should like you to read, but for the present I will content myself with saying, before all other books place the Word of God, which He has magnified above all His name. The Lord bless you, make you His children, and then Strict Baptists, and consistent members of gospel churches.

Your affectionate friend,

Brighton, February, 1920.   J. K. POPHAM.

2.

My dear Readers,—My last letter concluded by recommending you to read Biographies. Many display very remarkably the sovereign grace of God, and are worthy of your close attention. Who knows what the Spirit might accomplish in you by such reading!

Now I will go back to history. I desire that you may be made Strict Baptists. First, the children of God by regeneration; then brought into gospel liberty by a manifestation of the Lord Jesus and His blood and righteousness; then Baptists. Some may say they do not object to baptism, but Strict Communion they certainly are unable to believe is proper, seeing that many of the Lord's people are not Strict Baptists. I am not writing for controversy, nor in a controversial spirit; but let me ask you to notice *the* authority there is for Strict Communion. The history, in its commencement of such practice, is in the hands of you all. Turn to Matt. xxvi. 20—28; Mark xiv. 17—24; Luke xxii. 14—20. Later, the church numbered about a hundred and twenty. On the day of Pentecost, the Holy Ghost quickened and called, and added to the church and into church fellowship, " about three thousand souls." After this, churches were planted in many places by the apostles. All were Baptists. Here, then, is the authority.

for baptism and Strict Communion. Nobody questions this. With error of doctrine came error of practice in respect of baptism. I do not know of any small history of the Baptists which traces them from earliest sub-apostolic times to the present. There is one large "History of the Baptists; traced by their vital prin-ciples and practices from the time of our Lord and Saviour Jesus Christ to the year 1886," by Thomas Armitage. It is an American book, and not easy to obtain. Other works there are on this important subject —its mode and subjects, as Cramp, Carson, Ivimey and Norcott; but I think if you read carefully Philpot on "Strict Communion," you will obtain all necessary in-formation, and conviction will be carried even to your natural minds of the truth and scripturalness of our practice.

As you read, may the Spirit of truth open your eyes, that you may behold the wonders of truth; the beauty of gospel practice; and feel the power of both, and be found walking in them.

Your affectionate friend,

Brighton, March, 1920.   J. K. POPHAM.

3.

My dear young Friends,—This month I ask your attention to an important matter, a matter which, according to your attitude to it, will affect your lives for good or ill, since God in His all-wise providence works by means. The matter is in the word *Industry*. The Bible (which treats of all things relating to this our mortal life) deals with this very important matter. This you will readily see by the following passages: "Whatsoever thy hand findeth to do, do it with thy might; for there is no work, nor device, nor knowledge, nor wisdom, in the grave whither thou goest." "He becometh poor that dealeth with a slack hand; but the hand of the diligent maketh rich." "Seest thou a man diligent in his business? he shall stand before kings; he shall not stand before mean men." "Not slothful in business." "For when we were among you, this we commanded you, that if any man would not work, neither should he eat" (Eccles. ix. 10; Prov. x. 4; xxii. 29; Rom. xii. 11; 2 Thess. iii. 10). We then see that God in His Word puts an honour on labour when diligently attended to. And it is certainly a matter of common observation that He honours industry. Not in the same way in every individual instance, for many poor people, especially among the saints, do their utmost, and yet rarely do more than obtain the plainest living, but their industry is still honoured by God. This no doubt is sovereignly ordained for divinely wise ends. But it does not affect the general truth that ordinarily success follows diligence.

Now industry is first a matter of the mind. I use the word "mind" in the general sense of attention, purpose, disposition, and will. If a youth at school has no *mind* for his work, he may read and hear as much as any in the same form, but he will make no adequate progress; another, attending with all his mind, purposing to fit himself for a business or a profession, *will* hear, and read, and think; absorb and assimilate; and his progress is seen, and bears fruit. *Industry*, then, is not first in externals, but the disposition of the mind. In Ecclesiastes we see in the remarkable instance of Solomon the result of his attention to those matters which interested him. He acquainted his heart with wisdom. "I have made me great works; I builded me houses; I planted me vineyards." *His* was the *planning* mind; he gave his heart to it. His eye was on every object around him; he considered all things, and "he spoke three thousand proverbs; and his songs were a thousand and five. And he spake of trees, from the cedar that is in Lebanon even unto the hyssop that springeth out of the wall: he spake also of beasts, and of fowl, and of creeping things, and of fishes" (1 Kings iv. 32, 33). He did not merely see things without considering them. His mind, which God had given him, was exercised in and about all that came within his observation. So, I say to you, *do likewise*. Nothing will be drudgery, ignoble toil, which God in His providence puts to your hands, if your minds are engaged. You will see a dignity, a beauty in work. As poverty is no disgrace if it be in good company, so no kind of work can be said to be ignoble in itself. You may make it so to yourselves by improperly regarding it. Endeavour then to follow the divine direction, "Whatsoever thy hand findeth to do, do it with thy might."

Are you at school? Apply your whole mind to your daily tasks. Are you learning a business, or studying for a profession? Follow the same rule. *Observe detail.* Keep your eye on the top rung of the ladder, but never attempt two rungs at one step. Be sure of every step. Attempting too much, or seeking to attain to the top quickly would probably mean disaster, affecting all your life. *Use your time well;* use it in the evenings; be keepers at home. Do not seek much society. Avoid clubs. It is probable that club-life will sap, is sapping, much of the love of home-life, and the moral life of this country. *Read well.* I do not mean read many books, or read quickly, so much as read with the intention to understand, absorb, assimilate what you read, so that it shall become your own, your mental nourishment, strength, and equipment for your life. *Industry is real pleasure as well as profit.* Whoever looked with regret on his application to any subject? Do you fear God and seek His kingdom to come in your hearts? Read the divine direction given through Peter (2 Epistle i. 1—11), and the Lord give you understanding in all things.

Your affectionate friend,

March, 1922. J. K. POPHAM.

4.

My dear young Friends,—My best wishes to all of you for the New Year! What it will bring forth to the nation, to our families, and ourselves we know not. The merciful God hides to-morrow from us. But, to one and all of you, I say, God bless you—bless you with good health (the best of natural blessings), and give you wisdom to use it rightly, and to thank Him for it. It is a great help in work, whether you are preparing for trades or professions. Delicate health is a scotch on the wheels of industry, making work very hard. Youth is a ploughing and a sowing time; may you have health to cultivate; then, under God, you will reap a good harvest. I wish you may be prudent in your choice of friends. God alone knows how much depends on our friendships. We are influenced, and we influence. If sinners entice you, consent not. Do not connect yourselves with any whose language is not pure, or properly serious. Remember that it is said, " Evil communications corrupt good manners;" also remember that you must give an account for every idle word.

I desire you to consider, and have reverence for, authority. We are all under authority; it is inescapable. Authority is either original or delegated. We English people live under a delegated authority, and we are commanded to obey it. By divine inspiration the apostle Paul says, " Let every soul be subject to the higher powers. For there is no power but of God; the powers that be are ordained of God " (Rom. xiii. 1). Now God exercises His power in several ways. *In His Word.* Every commandment, every precept, every direction, given by the Spirit's inspiration, is absolute; no man can free himself from the duty of obedience. " Therefore shall ye observe all My statutes, and all My judgments " (Lev. xix. 37). I earnestly wish you all to observe this point. Do not forget that the Bible, being God's holy, infallible Word, has absolute authority over us all; over our hearts, minds and affections, claiming them for our Creator and Lawgiver; over our conduct towards our neighbour, commanding us to love him as ourselves. If this first great commandment be duly considered by us, we shall be convinced that we have never obeyed it. And if the conviction be by the Spirit of God, we shall be dead to the law by its action in us.

Then the Scriptures show us our many relative duties: " Honour thy father and mother, which is the first commandment with promise: that it may be well with thee, and thou mayest live long on the earth " (Eph. vi.

2, 3). It is sad to see so much disrespect, disobedience, and dishonour shown to parents now-a-days. Israel was taught how God regarded disobedience in children (read Deut. xxi. 19—21). What we owe to our neighbours is also clearly laid down in the Word of God: " Thou shalt not see thy brother's ox or his sheep go astray, and hide thyself from them: thou shalt in any case bring them again unto thy brother " (Deut. xxii. 1—4). Upright dealings with respect to all our transactions are laid on us as imperative duties. No unequal balance, no bag of deceitful weights are allowed (read Lev. xix. 36; Prov. xi. 1; xx. 23). Absolute honesty is thus laid on us. Servants must work honestly and earn their wages. Masters must pay proper wages, not exacting from their workmen more than they pay them for (Eph. vi. 5—9). Labour is our lot, the result of the Fall; there must be work of some kind done by all (Gen. iii. 17—19). Solemnly severe is the Lord against idleness (2 Thess. iii. 10). Becoming modesty in dress, and distinction of the sexes, are enjoined on us (Deut. xxii. 5). It is unspeakably sad and disgusting to see how immodestly many women and girls dress to-day. And in this connection I cannot be silent with regard to the awful fashion of a woman cutting off her hair. It is one of the strongest proofs that the Scriptures are not held in respect, that their authority is cast aside. What is woman's hair given her for ? For her covering and glory (1 Cor. xi. 6, 15). There the Holy Ghost says it is a shame for a woman to be shorn. Even nature teaches this. I hope my female readers will have no cause of offence with me for speaking thus.

In conclusion, I pray you all may very strictly in all things respect the inspired Word of God. Turn with abhorrence from the Modernist's teaching and declaiming against the inspiration of that divine Book. Shun his company, lest you be partakers of his plagues; for assuredly God will plague and punish him for taking away the inspiration of His Word; it is equal to taking away the whole Book. Oh, I wish you may be favoured to know that " the Word of God is quick and powerful,

and sharper than any two-edged sword, piercing even to
the dividing asunder of soul and spirit, and of the
joints and marrow, and is a discerner of the thoughts
and intents of the heart" (Heb. iv. 12). If in any of
you this mercy should be found during this year, you
will say, "O blessed 1926; that brought the living
Word of God to my heart by the Holy Ghost, who wrote
it in living characters on the fleshly table of my heart."

I can desire no greater blessing for my dear young
friends than the washing of regeneration and renewing
of the Holy Ghost. For that would be the appearing of
the kindness and love of God to you, would lead to
justification by His grace, and making you heirs according to the hope of eternal life (Tit. iii. 4—7).

I am, my dear young friends,
            Your affectionate friend,
Brighton, January, 1926.   J. K. POPHAM.

5.

My dear young Friends,—I greet you on this first day
of the New Year with the wish that Almighty God may
bless you all; keep you from evil; save you from sin,
and sinning; give you grace to confess and forsake sin;
for all who do so shall have mercy (Prov. xxviii. 13).

The opening of the New Year is an opportune
moment for a pause. The whirl of the present time,
the ever-pressing claims of business and pleasure leave
little time, and less inclination for pausing. Thinking
and moving furiously characterises this generation.
Reflection and introspection appears to be intolerable to
the majority of people. We are apparently *afraid* to
pause; everything, everybody demands speed. Whither
this furious driving is leading, men have no time to
inquire. The disposing, the guiding will and hand of
God, and the end of all things are left out of the
reckoning. There is no new thing under the sun (Jas.
iv. 13—15). Perhaps some who feel disposed to read
these lines are approaching the whirlpool. Study—so
full, so absorbing—will soon have to give place to business. New company, new surroundings, new temptations

must be met. May I ask you to *pause?* If you have godly parents, ask their advice; consider them in all your steps. If you are invited to meetings to which they, and you, are strangers, take counsel with them, and go in the way they direct. Remember also the wisdom of Solomon in the words, " My son, if sinners entice thee, consent thou not " (Prov. i. 10). It is good to observe it as viewed from a moral standpoint. Be most careful of your thoughts. They are mental pictures, and if they are evil, and are indulged in, you will soon have your eyes and your minds filled with evil pictures, and desires to realise them. Be careful of your language. Words follow and express thoughts. Loose words come from loose thinking. If money is entrusted to you, keep a strict account; never mix it with your own. Avoid gambling as you would avoid poison. It has often led to stealing. Keep away from clubs; let the society of the home-people suffice; have your recreation with them. Make good books your companions. Some of them will take you through your own beautiful country; others will show you foreign lands; others again, will interest you with word pictures of wonderful events, civil and ecclesiastical. Only readers know the pleasure, the refreshment and the enlargement of reading. How often has it driven away physical fatigue! But avoid fiction. It poisons thought. Be diligent in work. Give a good day's work for a good day's wage. This is but just. Avoid the gaping of the hireling for the shadow (Job vii. 2).

Thoughts and things fill up our short days; and if those thoughts and things are upright, it will be well for us and our neighbours. But all will be only as a shadow, a vapour, a weaver's shuttle. And if we are not God-fearing people, we spend our years under the thick cloud of His wrath (Ps. xc. 9). And yet so fascinated we may be with the passing events in which we are engaged and interested, we live as if listening to a well-told tale, oblivious to the time the narrative has occupied. How solemn is the import of the above passage! How soon shall we be carried away as with a flood! How soon will it be seen that our foundation is in the dust! "Man dieth, and wasteth away: yea, man giveth up the ghost, and where is he? As the waters fail from the sea, and the flood decayeth and drieth up: so man lieth down, and riseth not: till the heavens be no more, they shall not awake, nor be raised out, of their sleep. . . . If a man die shall he live again? All the days of my appointed time will I wait, till my change come " (Job xiv. 10—12, 14). The appointed time for the awakening by the Holy Ghost set forth by Paul: " For we must all appear before the judgment-seat of Christ: that every one may receive the things done in his body, according to that he hath done, whether it be good or bad " (2 Cor. v. 10). It is, then, solemn to live; it will be very solemn to die, and unspeakably solemn to appear before the Judgment-seat of Christ. The Lord help us to live, grant to us to die, *in Himself,* then shall we appear without shame before Him.

Your affectionate friend,

Brighton, January, 1921.   J. K. POPHAM.

6.

My dear young Friends,—Some of you are favoured still to possess both your parents, some may have lost one or the other, some may indeed have lost both, and to such I would extend my sympathy, for it is a loss indeed. Some of you may have had, or still have, parents who feared the Lord, and for this inestimable blessing you cannot be too thankful. What I would like to impress upon you now is the command given by God: " Children, obey your parents in all things: for this is well pleasing unto the Lord " (Col. iii. 20). This applies to all who are the *children* of their parents; it does not mean only those little ones of tender age, of whom we generally speak as " the children." It means them, and also those of maturer age, who do not think of themselves as " children," but who may perhaps feel very grown up, and quite able to manage their own affairs, so as scarcely to need the advice of parents! Oh, what a mistake this is! Only experience can teach some lessons, and in future years when you may be parents yourselves, you will look back upon your boyhood and girlhood days to see how wise were your parents when they exacted obedience on certain points where perhaps you had wished to act differently.

If you would save yourselves from bitter regrets then, be wise now in the days of your youth, and yield your will to that of your parents, believing that they know better than you.

If you would be favoured with the blessing of God, follow the example of some of your best friends, some of those whom you most admire, and be obedient to your parents. Remember it is the distinct command of God that you should be so; and that is quite sufficient, even if there were no promise beside. Some of you may be thoughtless and give your parents great trouble. Remember that it is from your heart the sin of disobedience, like all other sins, proceeds. May the Holy Spirit change your hearts, and make them anew! Then will you love God, and "honour your father and mother."

It has frequently been observed that the providence of God has been more strikingly evinced in reference to this commandment than any other. Few persons, who have not honoured their parents, have ever been known either to prosper in the world, or to live long in it. God has thus put the seal of His displeasure on such unnatural conduct.

But I believe this may not be the case with many, and perhaps not with any, of my dear young friends. Many of you I know from personal observation *are* obedient to your parents, you do "honour your father and your mother," and your loving conduct is a great comfort to them. Let me urge you not to relax in this as you grow older. *Go on* being good sons and daughters, and though you do not wish for reward, you will have it, for as we sow we reap, and the future will give you a peace of mind which is worth having. Though I think that however kind, obedient, gentle and unselfish you may be, you will never be satisfied that you have been all you might have been.

May God bless you, dear " children," young and old. Bless you in your homes, grant to you for many years the presence there of father and mother, bless you with the knowledge of your own sinfulness, and bless you with the blessing of forgiven sin, sin put away by the atoning Sacrifice of the Lord Jesus Christ. Then you will be blest indeed. Seek it for yourselves, and may the Holy Spirit enable you to " seek and find."

Your affectionate friend,

Brighton, July, 1923. J. K. POPHAM.

7.

My dear young Friends,—This month's letter is to be about a very great and highly important subject. The subject is embodied in a short word, a word which, because it is in common use, and also because we may have no special need to notice it, we do not reflect on it. Close observation of words and things seems, as a rule, only to be aroused by some sort of necessity. But observation of all things is profitable, both naturally and spiritually. It is a sin not to observe the operation of God's hand (Ps. xxviii. 5). You may gather much useful knowledge by close observation, and get an education by *reading* words. If you go for a holiday, and can take only two books, take your Bible and a dictionary. The Bible *may* be made spirit and life— eternal life—to you; the dictionary you will always find instructive and useful. Our cursive life is not gainful.

Well, the little word I wish you to *read* with me is the common word SOBER. It is not the monster of Greek mythology having many heads, but though, according to the dictionary, a word of uncertain origin, is certainly a word of simple and clear application. It is quite a common word, and so *generally* understood, that perhaps we may be excused if we have given it little or no attention. We speak of a sober-minded youth in opposition to a light, trifling person; a sober, thoughtful, sane, all-round, reasoned view of matters, as opposed to a hasty, ill-informed, prejudiced, one-sided view. Such sober-mindedness as above leads to a corresponding walk, to an attempt, at least, to do justice to men whose words or conduct may be impugned.

Let us then look at our word " sober."

1. It is taken as the opposite to excessive indulgence in intoxicating liquors. You are arriving, or have arrived, at an age when you will necessarily go more into the world than hitherto; when you will meet with examples and teachings other than those of home; when your receptive, susceptible minds will be exposed to temptations. You will probably see excessive drinking —a terrible, national sin. In that case may the Lord help you to remember and believe and follow His inspired word: " Who hath woe ? who hath sorrow ? who hath contentions ? who hath babblings ? who hath wounds without cause ? who hath redness of eyes ? They that tarry long at the wine; that go to seek mixed wine. Look not thou upon the wine when it is red, when it giveth his colour in the cup, when it moveth itself aright. At the last it biteth like a serpent, and stingeth like an adder " (Prov. xxiii. 29—31). Aim, then, to seek ever to abstain from, to be sober in respect of, the excessive use of strong drink. Think of the ruin it constantly brings to innumerable families in the land. It is perhaps impossible to say how much of Solomon's transgression was the result of giving himself to wine (Ecc. ii. 3), but his mind and judgment might have been so affected and warped that falling into idolatry was comparatively easy, especially when under the intoxicating, godless influence of " outlandish women." Avoid the sparkling cup. *Be sober.* Let your moderation be known unto all men in this important respect.

2. Be *sober*, without enthusiasm, in your choice of friends. A suggestion of improper conduct of any kind on the part of one who would be your friend should be sufficient to warn, admonish, and prevent you from forming a friendship to which you might be inclined. Turn from youths who indulge in slangy expressions about their parents and sisters, whose ideas of honesty

F

are not strict, who are disposed to break the Sabbath, to speak slightingly of the Bible, whose principles are lax respecting capital and labour. Their relation and inter-dependence are essential, for the destruction of either would inevitably involve the death of the other. If any of you become masters, *be careful,* make it a matter of conscience to pay a just, yea, a liberal wage; and to those of you who will be employees, I earnestly say, make it a matter of conscience to give a fair day's work for a fair day's wage. From those who would keep you from your home in the evening, turn away. Remember the Holy Scripture which speaks thus: " My son, if sinners entice thee, consent thou not. . . . My son, walk not thou in the way with them; refrain thy foot from their path. For their feet run to evil, and make haste to shed blood " (Prov. i. 10—16). It may be regarded as a good maxim that our *chosen* companions may be taken as an index to our minds. The influence of company, companionship, is very subtle, not gross, but thin, like a gas, insinuating itself through the crevices of our minds. For our minds are not without fissures. And the arch tempter knows it. He found that with Eve. She was not invulnerable, but he would not give her a sudden shock by a bold declaration against God, so suggested that probably she had not a clear under-standing of the commandment. In such a way a would-be friend may gently insinuate a thought, a matter which you would know was evil if boldly stated. Oh, *be sober in your friendships.*

3. *Be sober* in your dress. Do not imitate the youth who is vain of dress, the fop. Foppishness comes from an empty mind. That style of dress which would attract attention, the friendly, approving attention of vain persons, the scornful attention of desirable people, avoid.

4. Be sober, discriminating in your choice of books. Works on your professions and businesses you *must* have, and they, of course, will not necessarily lead you astray with respect to your morals. But shun works of fiction. The moral and physical damage they have

wrought and are working will, perhaps, not be fully known in this world.

I must close abruptly, having meant to say more on this head. May a word to the wise be sufficient!

Your affectionate friend,

Brighton, April, 1925.   J. K. Popham.

8.

My dear young Friends,—Our meditation this month shall be on the important words, " Blessed is the man that walketh not in the counsel of the ungodly, nor standeth in the way of sinners, nor sitteth in the seat of the scornful " (Ps. i. 1). Here is a gradation, a movement from a state of mind to an act, from an act to a continuance of the act, a satisfaction in it. Sin is not, in all its forms and degrees, generated and completed at once. From its conception to its finish it is one in its *nature*, but its degrees and developments may be distinctly marked, definitely distinguished (Jas. i. 14, 15). " Blessed " some translate, " Oh the blessedness or happiness of the man that walketh not in the counsel of the ungodly." Counsel is advice, direction, suggestion. All that is *intended* is not on the surface. " Counsel in the heart of man is like deep water " (Prov. xx. 5). One who entices to sin will not open at once all his purpose to the simple one who is heeding his wicked counsel. By degrees the purpose is made known. It is like " the wine when it is red, when it giveth his colour in the cup, when it moveth itself aright." The intoxication contained in the enticing cup is not suspected or feared. The lurking danger lies hidden in the glistening sparkle. So the counsel of the ungodly is to gain consent of the will. And the attention given, the " walking " in the counsel is the destroying result. It leads to " standing in the way of sinners." The evil communication has corrupted good manners. The fear of sinning, if not entirely destroyed, is very greatly weakened. Conscience has lost its authority, if it murmur a protest its voice is not heeded. The man " stands in the counsel " of evil men; he is past the counsel of the tempter, he is in the way the counsellor pointed out. He consents to sin, he commits it in the company of sinners, in the broad way that leadeth to destruction. The next step in the terrible gradation indicates a continuance and a satisfaction in sin. The man "sits with scorners," and he will not heed rebuke, he stretches out his hand with other scorners.

The man who escapes this snare of the devil is a blessed man. It is only "the abhorred of the Lord" who shall be taken in it and never escape, to whom sin shall not appear exceeding sinful. As the forbidden fruit was made to appear pleasant to Eve and a food to be desired, by the counsel of the serpent, she quickly stood in the way of the chief sinner. It is so to-day. Evil communications corrupt good manners. They first corrupt the stream of thought, then that appears good which is deadly evil, the seductive appearance is powerful, action follows.

What is the blessedness of not being found in the threefold evil of our verse ?

i. It lies in the possession of eternal life, the fear of the Lord, and the gracious teaching and prompting of the Holy Ghost. The great evil of the counsel of the ungodly is seen. "So did not I because of the fear of God." The awful counsel of the ungodly critic of to-day may come to the reflective mind of a true child of God, but the authority, the life, light and power of the Word in the hand of the Spirit will preserve him from walking, standing, sitting in so evil and deadly a thing.

ii. It consists in the spirit of prayer and the grace of supplications. "Open Thou mine eyes that I may behold wondrous things out of Thy law." "And Jabez called on the God of Israel, saying, Oh that Thou wouldest bless me indeed, and enlarge my coast, and that Thine- hand might be with me, and that Thou wouldest keep me from evil, that it may not grieve me! And God granted him that which he requested" (1 Chron. iv. 10).

iii. It is in the faith of God's elect, of His operation,

which brings the needy soul, sensible of its exposedness, its hourly danger, to cast itself on the death, burial, resurrection and intercession of Christ for "safety on earth, and after death the plenitude of heaven."

iv. It is in the blessed unction from the Holy One, who brings and fixes in the heart the truth which " dwelleth in us, and shall be with us for ever."

v. It is in the love of God, from which nothing can separate. And when that precious love is shed abroad in the heart by the Holy Ghost, life, light, peace and strength are within and make the heart strong. Thus a young man cleanses his way by taking heed thereto according to God's word (Ps. cxix. 9).

This being a brief meditation on the blessedness of a true Christian man, I would fain hope and desire that that inestimable good might be the sovereignly designed, the invincibly gracious gift of God to my young friends. It has no parallel in time, as time has no parallel in eternity. Oh, the terribleness of being accursed of God for our sins! the fearfulness of being abhorred of the Lord for our sins! Oh, the blessedness of possessing His freely-given eternal life, eternal redemption, eternal Spirit! Thus favoured, and thus only, can any sinner escape the snare of the fowler. And thus may my readers be " blessed."

Your affectionate friend,

Brighton, September, 1925.   J. K. POPHAM.

9.

My dear young Friends,—A correspondent has suggested to me that it might be profitable to write to you about the shameful way in which some women and girls dress to-day. Also, he gives me a text, or rather, two passages of Scripture from which to preach; and I am disposed to adopt his suggestion and make the two portions of the Word of God the basis of my remarks. The passages are these: " The woman shall not wear that which pertaineth unto a man, neither shall a man put on a woman's garment: for all that do so are abomination unto the Lord thy God " (Deut. xxii. 5).

Speaking of prayer made by men, the Apostle writes:
" I will therefore that men pray everywhere, lifting up
holy hands, without wrath and doubting. In like
manner also, that women adorn themselves in modest
apparel, with shamefacedness and sobriety; not with
broided hair, or gold, or pearls, or costly array; but
(which becometh women professing godliness) with
good works " (1 Tim. ii. 9, 10). This divinely commanded distinction of the sexes, in their respective
habiliments, has its rise in their creation as male and
female: " So God created man in His own image, in the
image of God created He him "—here is human nature
in the collective sense—" male and female created He
them." This created difference is manifested and declared by their dress. After the Fall, and the idolatry
to which man, led of the god of this world, became
addicted, disguises were assumed, men wearing women's
dress, and women putting on men's, according to the
supposed sex of their idols. It is said that the custom
became extensively prevalent. This, of course, led to
the indecent levities practised in common life. Hence
from the idolatrous changes of raiment, the evil custom
spread to civil life. Thus a religious and moral principle became involved, and all who practised the forbidden disguise, or ignored the created sex difference,
were an abomination to God (Deut. xxii. 5). The chosen
nation must not conform to idolatrous custom. So
neither must spiritual Israel conform to the world.

Two things are forbidden to women in the church of
God. (a) Cutting off the hair. Their hair is given them
for a covering and glory. Every professing woman dishonours herself by having her hair cut off, except in case
of sickness, and then only remaining short until re-
covery. She sins against God, removes her God-given
veil, and disqualifies herself for communion. (b) Inor-
dinately gay or costly dress. They are to be modestly
attired. Not to broider their hair with gold; a custom
of intertwining gold with the plaiting of the hair.
Thus the love of fine dress is rebuked and forbidden
by the Spirit of God to the saints. They are not of the

world, therefore they must be different from it. Christ redeemed them from the present evil world; and in His prayer for them, would have them sanctified by the truth of the gospel. Every woman professing godliness should be a living protest against the immodest mode of dressing to-day. To all to whom this letter is written I say: Bear in mind the words of the Holy Ghost by the Apostle Paul: "In like manner that women adorn themselves in modest apparel." Turn away, with a proper disgust, from the almost-nude girl, or those who adopt as far as possible the attire of man.

The Lord God of Abraham, Isaac, and Jacob make you Jews inwardly, and enable you to walk according to the light of the blessed gospel.

Your affectionate friend,

Brighton, November, 1930. J. K. POPHAM.

10.

My dear young Friends,—My few words about " bobbed hair " have brought me some letters of approval and disapproval, the former and the latter written very kindly. I thank my correspondents. Now, as the Word of God, our only infallible guide, speaks of woman's hair, and the purpose for which it is given her, and as many of my friends are really concerned about the important matter, I propose dealing more precisely and fully with it than was possible in my almost incidental remarks. The subject may occupy two letters, but it is too important from the Scripture point to be content with mere assertions. It is just because the Word of God tells us His mind about it, that it is proper for a man to express an opinion. If only fashion, or health, or other personal reasons, not touched or disallowed by the Scriptures, were the dominating factors, let all masculine objectors be silent. But such is not the case. The Lord has spoken, let all the earth keep silence. From His Word there is no appeal. There is no option left where that Word pronounces judgment. A thing is right or wrong, just as the Bible declares. Time, circumstances, personal predilections have no standing, no voice here, nothing is allowed but obedience, conformity to the revealed will of God. Grandly and beautifully does Luther speak of the Word of God: "Let us hold it for certain and firmly established that the soul can do without everything except the Word of God, without which none of its wants are provided for. But, having the Word, it is rich and wants for nothing, since it is the word of life, of truth, of light, of liberty, of wisdom, of virtue, of grace, of glory, and of every good thing." With the conviction that the above comprehensive description of Holy Scripture is true, true for all time, and the subject before us is an integral part of the divine Word, let us attend to what is there said about it.

"But every woman that prayeth or prophesieth with her head uncovered dishonoureth her head; for that is even all one as if she were shaven. . . . But if a woman have long hair, it is a glory to her; for her hair is given her for a covering" (1 Cor. xi. 5—15). It is well known that into the Corinthian church irregularities had come, and marred the worship and beauty of the services, and invaded doctrine. Indeed, all irregularities in worship or practice will be found ultimately to touch doctrine. Peter's defection reflected on the doctrine of justification (Gal. ii. 11—16). So the unseemly manner of the women praying and prophesying in the church at Corinth violated their fundamental subjection to man. Before reproving the faulty manner of female worship, the apostle ascends to the source of all propriety. Generally, the Corinthians kept the ordinances as he had delivered them to them, but there were particular instances of departure from a due observance of them. And the first to be censured was the unveiling of women in public worship, which was the removal of the token of her subordination to man, "But," says the apostle, "I would have you know, that the head of every man is Christ; and the head of the woman is the man; and the head of Christ is God." Thus the history of the creation of woman proclaims her subjection. For a man to pray or prophesy, having his head covered, dishonoureth his head. " For a man indeed ought not to cover his head, forasmuch as he is the image and glory of God." Not so with the woman. For while there is an equality in *nature,* and a mutual dependence between man and woman, " for neither is without the other," in *relation* the woman is subject to the man. And the mark of this is her veil, and from that outward mark, which may and does vary in different nations, her hair remains, for it is her *natural* glory and covering. This is so self evident that the apostle appeals even to the judgment of the church on it: " Judge in yourselves: is it comely that a woman pray unto God uncovered ? Doth not even nature itself teach you, that, if a man have long hair, it is a shame unto him ? But if a woman have long hair, it is a glory to her: for her hair is given her for a covering." This divine pronounce- ment is so positive, it is a wonder that any God-fearing woman or young girl can entertain a doubt about the sin of cutting off her hair. When the inspired Word of God says a certain thing is shameful, surely dishonour must attach to the person who does it. Where the Scripture has its proper authority by the inward work- ings of the Inspirer of it, such a shameful thing will ever be impossible. For it will be seen that the evil interferes with *worship, a fundamental doctrine.* I therefore must adhere to my expressed hope (is it a well grounded hope ?) that none of our ministers will administer the Lord's Supper to one who has despised, or at least forgotten, the Scripture which tells her she has done a shameful thing in cutting off her glory and covering. Oh that we might be given really to believe in the inspiration of the Bible! Then we should agree with Paul, or rather with God who says by Paul, that the divine Volume " is profitable for doctrine, for re- proof, for correction, for instruction in righteousness: that the man of God may be perfect, throughly fur- nished unto all good works " (2 Tim. iii. 16, 17).

My letter has reached its limit, and I therefore must leave several points touched on by my correspondents in connection with the subject for my next letter, if the

Lord will. Consider what the Scripture says, and the Lord give you understanding in all things.

Your affectionate friend,

Brighton, October, 1926.   J. K. POPHAM.

11.

My dear young Friends,—In my last letter I set before you what the Bible says about woman's hair, that it is given her for a glory and a covering. Let me here remind you that the Word of God is settled for ever in heaven (Ps. cxix. 89). What was written in the Psalmist's day is true to-day. Doctrine, promise, precept, statute, direction had no more authority then than now. They will continue to be believed, held, loved, followed and obeyed to the end of time. And it is a solemn thing to break one word of God. " Whosoever therefore shall break one of these least commandments, and shall teach men so, he shall be called the least in the kingdom of heaven " (Matt. v. 17—19). The breaker of a jot or tittle of either law, gospel, or the " new commandment," dishonours God in that particular, and will find that he is dishonoured of God. Pause here, then, and reflect on the sin of disregarding 1 Cor. xi. 5—16. Surely this solemn teaching, this *abiding* word should make a God-fearing, Bible-reading woman, who has cut off her glory, weep for shame and resolve at once to let it grow, and seek for forgiveness for violating the Scripture and dishonouring herself.

The Holy Ghost teaches that the evil practice of cutting off the hair of a woman touches the fundamental of divine worship. " Is it comely that a woman pray unto God uncovered ? " This is a *principle*. Her attire may alter, will differ in different countries, but her *natural* covering cannot properly be removed without affecting her worship. Her action is " uncomely," unseemly. How deeply this will affect all who have *thus* dishonoured themselves when they see the matter in the light of the Spirit's teaching! For to worship God truly in " due order " is the desire of His children. It is a matter of conscience, faith, and love. To be right in secret and public worship is most important; and any disregard to the Scripture direction in the matter is dishonouring to the only Object of true (that is, spiritual) worship.

As some of my correspondence on the subject of " bobbed " hair contains various pleas for it, I must notice one or two of them. i. It is said *that short hair is more healthy.* Well, I have yet to learn and believe that God made a mistake when He gave woman her glory; nay, more, that He was unkind. For being God only wise He knew that long hair would be detrimental to health! What a reflection is that plea on the beneficent Creator! A reflection of a carnal mind, of a corrupted reason. I ask you all to consider this seriously. But *doctors order it to be cut off,* just as they amputate a limb, but that is done in disease, not in health, not in the *natural* state of things. ii. Another plea is *that it is much more comfortable to have short hair than the long hair which nature has given.* That of course is a matter of personal feeling, but as a *plea* it is against the Bible. God made Eve of Adam and gave her long hair, and whatever feeling about comfort there may be it must not weigh against the wisdom and goodness in which He acted in making her what she is. Comfort against the Creator—never! iii. Yet a third plea is, *it is easier to keep short hair clean and tidy than long hair.* Again a personal feeling, and seeming convenience against nature. That is to say, set the Word of God aside to suit an *unnatural* disposition. To all the above, and much more, I have one word to say—the Bible, the Bible, the Bible! What saith the Scripture ? " To the law and to the testimony: if they speak not according to this word, it is because there is no light (morning, margin) in them " (Isa. viii. 20).

But an appeal is made to the words of the Holy Ghost in the passage which treats of this subject. After " very careful study " one correspondent arrived at the conclusion that the word " nature " in verse 14 means " custom." But if the infallible Teacher had intended custom in that verse, would He not have used the same

word as we find in verse 16 ? But He inspired His
servant Paul to employ two different words because He
was treating of two different things. The word our
Bible has for nature in verse 14 is also used in Rom. ii.
14, 27; xi. 24; Gal. ii. 15, and iv. 8. The word means
just what all understand, that which belongs to our
nature. It is natural for Gentiles to do the things contained in the law, for they are " written in their hearts."
Uncircumcision is natural, circumcision is a covenant
obligation restricted to the Jews. A wild olive branch
is naturally such, if it becomes a fruitful branch it is so
by being " grafted contrary to nature into a good olive
tree." The word *custom* in verse 16 of our subject
simply means common usage, and common usage here
means that the shameful practice of some women in the
church at Corinth was not customary in the " churches
of God." The custom of those churches is the custom
of every gospel church to-day. And wherever the Word
of God has authority in the conscience by the Holy
Ghost that godly practice or custom will be found. It
can only be regarded as a sad sign of the lack of
gracious experience, and of a proper knowledge of the
Bible, that any professing woman has felt to be so much
her own as to do what is forbidden her. The good Lord
restore everyone who has thus transgressed!

I have noticed the immodest short dress, low neck,
and bare arms. Having directed how the men should
pray, the apostle speaks of the deportment and dress of
women: " That women adorn themselves in modest
apparel, with shamefacedness and sobriety; not with
broidered hair, gold, or pearls, or costly array; but
(which becometh women professing godliness) with good
works " (1 Tim. ii. 9). Peter was inspired to write on
the same important subject. " . . . Whose adorning let
it not be that outward adorning of plaiting the hair
(usually with gold; it must have been long), and of
wearing of gold, or of putting on of apparel."

Thus we see that the Word of God gives ample
guidance to us for our conduct, dress, and worship.
And where it is carefully read, and has authority in the

conscience, there will be conformity to it, to its divine doctrines, its heavenly teachings, its holy forbiddings, its gracious and distinct directions.

God bless you all with a respect for, a true faith in, a humble obedience to, His divine Word, and thus keep you from the unseemly, dishonourable fashions of this "evil world," and give you an experience of an interest in Christ's prayer (John xvii. 17).

Your affectionate friend,
Brighton, November, 1926.   J. K. POPHAM.

12.

My dear young Friends,—Owing to pressure of work and a little overtiredness, I am unable to write my monthly letter to you. This note is just to tell you I have not forgotten you, and that I wish for you that blessing of the Lord which maketh rich and addeth no sorrow therewith. Three words I wish to say to you. i. *Avoid trashy, bad reading.* The temptation is very great. Bookstalls, libraries, stationers' shops, are so many temptations: novels are displayed everywhere, and probably you will see them in the hands of your school friends and have the loan of them offered you. Shun them. There are plenty of interesting facts in histories, read them; they will store your minds without polluting them or exciting them to evil things. ii. *Avoid places of amusement, so-called.* Cinemas are a terrible evil. Never go inside one of them. How many young people have been led, or driven by excitement, to the first step in dishonesty by attending what can be called dens of evil. Spend your spare time in your homes, or in healthy walks. iii. *Keep the Lord's day.* Go to your chapels with your parents, then read the Bible, the only infallible Book. It tells us of our creation, of our sin, of the divinely provided remedy in and by Jesus, and of the Holy Ghost, who alone is able to give new life and saving knowledge of the Lord Jesus Christ.

God bless you all,
Your affectionate friend,
Brighton, June, 1930.   J. K. POPHAM.

13.

My dear young Friends,—The holy Word of God
says, " My son, if sinners entice thee, consent thou not "
(Prov. i. 10). Read the whole chapter. The counsel is
most pure and wholesome and much to be regarded and
pondered over. " If sinners entice thee," does not mean
that the enticed one is not a sinner; for all are sinners.
It means that openly wicked men and women come to
one who is moral and of good behaviour, and seek to
draw him into some sin or sins, into conduct contrary to
the instruction of his father and the law of his mother
(ver. 8). They had doubtless warned him against open
sin, laid him under parental authority, pointed out to
him the commandment of God with regard to loving
and obeying them (Exod. xx. 12; Matt. xv. 4). The
son was thus, as we to-day would say, " Well brought
up." And Jewish law with regard to the subjection of
children and obedience to their parents was very strict
(Deut. xxi. 21). To-day we have run to the mad
extreme. Parental authority is very largely unknown.
The commandment of God to children in regard to their
parents is ignored. May God keep you tender, loving
and obedient to your parents, and help you to regard
the precept: " If sinners entice thee, consent thou not."
" If thy brother . . . entice thee secretly " (Deut. xiii.
6), such would be the case with you if enticed. Sinners
would take care not to endeavour to persuade you to
commit an open sin in the presence of your parents; the
persuasion would be in secret. They would meet you
in the street and walk with you from school or your
place of business. You attend a place of worship on
Lord's days with your parents, and the bondage of it,
the pleasure of a country walk with good companions
might be an early counsel, working in you a dislike to
the keeping of the Lord's day. Oh, consent not! The
cinema would be another enticement—so lively, exciting,
full of fun—perhaps an offer of paying for you the
first visit to such a way to hell. Oh, consent not!
Police Court reports tell of the evil influence of such

terribly wicked places. Bad company, nightly walks, encouraging you to disobey your father's rule that you should be home by such an hour, infusing a defiant spirit of rebellion against him, and making home an unpleasant place, exciting in your depraved nature much evil. Oh, consent not! You have a depraved nature, latent lusts. May God keep you from the match which would set them ablaze: " If sinners entice thee, consent thou not." The enticement might be to taste strong drink. " Look not thou upon the wine when it is red, when it giveth his colour in the cup, when it moveth itself aright. At the last it biteth like a serpent, and stingeth like an adder " (Prov. xxiii. 31, 32). The enticer may be a novel reader. He may offer to lend you a book which he says is very interesting, not very exciting, but it is enough to beget in you a desire to read another, and another. You cannot allow your parents to see the pernicious stuff, so you with deceit smuggle it in and hide it in some place from their eyes. You read novels till the desire becomes a passion, a fire in your heart. Oh, consent not! The beginning of sins, this among them, is like the letting out of water. Who can bound the issues thereof ? (Prov. xvii. 14.) A tempter may be a gambler, a card-player. No stakes at the first, lest you should be shocked and the hook should not take. Later on, a small stake and you are allowed to win. The success you have draws to further ventures, you lose, you get into debt, opportunity to steal (temporarily you think), and thus you sink, moral feeling is killed, or at least wounded, stunned, and scarcely able to breathe a regret. Oh, consent not! my dear young friends, if you are enticed. You have the same fallen nature as the enticers. Go not in the way with them.

May the God of all grace look on you and save you from sinning, and from sin; give you grace to fear His great and holy Name, and to walk in His ways.

Your affectionate friend,

Brighton, May, 1932.   J. K. POPHAM.

14.

My dear young Friends,—It is painfully trite to say we are living in bad, evil, perilous times; but, though it is so trite, it is also terribly true. The days *are* bad, hurtful, against God's commandments, and therefore perilous, full of danger. For Divine threatenings are against the things which are prevailing among us. Yet the practices which are prevalent are perilous because attractive to our nature. Take, for example, the rebuilding of the Buckfast Abbey, and the approving descriptions of the opening ceremonies by the so-called Cardinal Bourne. What did it all mean but the advertising of the blasphemous Roman Catholic religion? The wonderful monks, who doffed their religious (?) garbs and became stone-masons and builders, and patiently worked for years to build and beautify the Abbey. The much advertised reopening, the gorgeously-apparelled cardinal and bishops and priests. It was only dressing up the whore of Babylon in order to allure poor, foolish Protestants, saying to them, "You have been taught that our religion is a dark and evil system; you have been deceived. See what these self-denying men have accomplished; listen to our beautiful intoning, see our reverent worship." And the press of this country, much of which is, alas! under popish control, took great pains to embellish the whole with highest praise. Yet, let me tell you, all this was nothing but dressing beautifully a leper, and sending him to walk among the people, an attraction and invitation to Protestants to receive the mark of the beast in their foreheads and hands. So is the present state of our nation and the world, perilous. It is different from matters of my youth, though they were truly sufficiently evil. But the Victorian days had character and a standard of morals which is generally sneered at to-day.

Of two evils, which prevail to-day, I wish to warn you. i. *Sabbath-breaking*. It is universal. The flagrant disregard of the day of rest must bring judgment on individuals, communities, and nations indulging in it. Be warned, be careful not to desecrate the Lord's day. On the seventh day God rested from His work of creation. On the Lord's day Jesus rested from His work of redemption. Never do any unnecessary work, or indulge in any games, or read any book that would turn you from the Bible. If sinners entice you to break the Lord's day, consent not. Attend where the gospel is preached, and may God bless the preaching to you, give you saving repentance toward God, and faith toward our Lord Jesus Christ. Oh, that would be a blessing indeed, ending in an everlasting rest or Sabbath. ii. *Do not indulge in the games of the day,* or go to cinemas or theatres. Of games it may be said there is no harm in tennis or cricket. True, if no more is intended than hitting a ball with racket or a bat, but it is the company you may be drawn into, the snares to which the games may expose you. You may be led to gambling. You may be invited to meetings which would taint your morals and make sin little in your eyes; you may hear language which would, perhaps, at the first shock you, but you would soon become accustomed to the sounds and indulge in them. If any of you make a profession, and are really the children of the Most High God (Prov. i. 10), I specially entreat you to avoid the dangerous snares. Follow the old saints you may know. Never listen to any disparaging remarks concerning them. Rise up at the hoary head. Listen to their conversation about their trials, their conflicts with sin and Satan, and their helps, mercies and comforts. So doing, you will be kept from the snares, games, and bad company. Remember Solomon's saying: "He that walketh with wise men shall be wise; but a companion of fools shall be destroyed" (Prov. xiii. 20). Also the good word of Peter, "Honour all men. Love the brotherhood. Fear God. Honour the king" (1 Pet. ii. 17). Thus blest by the Lord you will come through all evil example, and at last be where no sin is, either in yourselves or the blessed heaven prepared for all elected and redeemed and regenerated souls.

With all good wishes, dear young friends, I am,
                    Your affectionate friend,
Brighton, October, 1932.   J. K. POPHAM.

15.

My dear young Friends,—Let us consider for a few minutes the solemn and important words of the Holy Ghost, " Speak ye every man the truth to his neighbour " (Zech. viii. 16). Untruthfulness in any form is what God hates (ver. 17; Prov. vi. 17). It is deceit, consciously saying what is known to be false with intent to cover an evil (Ezek. xiii. 19). It is speaking against, departing from the Lord (Isa. lix. 13). Thus we see in Holy Scripture how great a sin lying is. It may be direct, as when the serpent deceived Eve, saying to her, " Ye shall not surely die," a direct contradiction to God who had said *death* should follow transgression. But the enemy had craftily prepared the ear of Eve by insinuations (Gen. iii. 1—4). It may be that a person suddenly, without premeditation, utters a falsehood, as Peter did when he denied any knowledge of his Lord and Saviour. But though his first lie was the result of a sudden and powerful inflowing of fear and cowardice, the second and third denials were deliberate (Matt. xxvi. 71—75). A lie may be told to cover a previous sin (Prov. x. 18); but God will deal with liars, unless, as in Peter's case, He gives repentance (Ps. xxxi. 18; Rev. xxi. 27).

By the above Scriptures, my young friends, may you see the greatness, the wickedness, the guilt, and the punishment of lying. May your hearts be touched by the sight. There are many temptations to untruthfulness, and some people are more naturally disposed to the sin than others. Youth is open to the evil. A wrong done to parents or a friend, and the temptation to cover it by denying it. May all of you be made sensible of the sin of saying what is not true in any shape or form. Flee from it as from a fire, which fleeing will often bring you quietness and peace; as from a serpent, whose poison will gnaw your conscience as long as you live, even if you have grace and forgiveness. Be afraid of the hardening effects of lying, the deceitfulness of sin is hardness. Indulged untruthfulness begets deadness to the evil. A friend of mine (now dead) who had lived in the east, and had dealings with Arabs, told me that a proverb among them was, " Lying is the salt of a man." Oh! in your youth fear the dreadful habit of the sin of lying. The Spirit of God says by Solomon, " The lip of truth shall be established for ever; but a lying tongue is but for a moment " (Prov. xii. 19). Ever seek a clean tongue, then you will fear no man as regards your words. The blessing of the Lord, which maketh rich and addeth no sorrow therewith, rest on you all.

Your affectionate friend,

Brighton, June, 1933.   J. K. POPHAM.

16.

My dear young Friends,—The Psalmist, desiring to honour God in His Word, says to Him, " Thy Word is very pure: therefore Thy servant loveth it " (Ps. cxix. 140). It would be well if such a view of the Bible were in all of us. One result would be a reverence for it, a desire to walk according to it. We should be afraid of being contrary to it, and tremble at it. We should desire to shelter within its promises, in the loving embrace of its doctrine, under the smile and blessing of its divine Author. Heresies have ever plagued, darkened, blackened, and degraded men who have professed the name of God; to a terrible degree it is so to-day. And perhaps, one of the worst heresies now rife among religious people is that of the blatant repudiation of the Bible as plenarily inspired, and therefore binding on men, demanding from them full submission of their whole being to God, their Creator and Lawgiver. The eyes of many are almost exclusively on Popery. It is indeed an unmitigated evil, an arrant and a daily blasphemy, the abomination which maketh desolate. But does not the rejection of the Bible as God's most pure, most wonderful, entirely infallible Word, cast the most awful reflection on Him and make desolate a person, a church, a community, a nation, where it prevails? How the Lord looks on the rejection of His Word, we see in Jer. vi. 19, and viii. 9. Think on this aspect of the case, of the guilt, and the punishment which follows, in the blindness which He inflicts, and the madness, and, if repentance and faith be not given, what must be the everlasting lot of such people?

There is one word in the Bible I want you to look at with me for a few moments; to regard it as being full of divine authority, as showing how odious to God must that be which He forbids. The word is as follows: " Thou shalt not go up and down as a talebearer among thy people: neither shalt thou stand against the blood of thy neighbour: I am the Lord " (Lev. xix. 16). The reprehensible habit of talebearing is an old one, and evidently an offence against God. The above passage was given as a law quite early in the national life of Israel, given to shape their social conduct, to regulate their neighbourly intercourse. It was a necessary and wholesome law. For the Lord knew that " the tongue is a fire, a world of iniquity, so is the tongue among our members, that it defileth the whole body, and setteth on fire the course of nature; and it is set on fire of hell. . . . The tongue can no man tame; it is an unruly evil, full of deadly poison " (Jas. iii. 6, 8).

Against this evil habit of talebearing and speaking as busybodies in other men's matters, I would warn you. Solomon tells us " the words of a talebearer are as wounds; and they go down into the innermost parts (chambers, margin) of the belly." Also that " He that goeth about as a talebearer revealeth secrets " (Prov. xviii. 8; xx. 19). By the Apostle Paul the Holy Ghost puts talebearers among disorderly persons, calling them busybodies, and calls them to order; he joins the practice to idleness.

Now, because the Word of God condemns this vicious habit, I am sure it becomes us all to endeavour to avoid it. Whatever the Scripture condemns is evil. On this ground, then, in the first place do abstain from what, alas, is so common. Then also, because it is a wound to someone's character. Be careful of the character of your friends and acquaintances. Observe this care in the Lord Jesus. You will find it in a word which we may not have noticed with any special care: " Judas saith unto Him, *not Iscariot.*" Two men, bearing the same name, about Christ, one betrayed his Master, the other was a true servant of His: so when John was writing his gospel, Christ said by His Spirit, " Distinguish Judas the brother of James from the betrayer of Christ." Here is an example left; may grace be given us to be careful of the character of a friend or acquaintance. An effectual method of dealing with a talebearer is to say to him, " Now what you wish to say against my friend I shall repeat to him." I have found such a plan to work well, and quickly relieve me of the company of the obnoxious person. (See Matt. xviii. 15, 16.) Finally, remember that you must give an account of every idle word. Oh, what an alarming word has that been to some! If you defame a person's character, you not only wound and injure him, but you inflict a more deadly wound on your own consciences. God in time and by providence may abundantly vindicate the injured character, but only the blood of Christ can cleanse and heal you. Shun the evil and the doers of it.

The Almighty and ever gracious God bless you all.

Your affectionate friend and well-wisher,

Brighton, August, 1922.   J. K. POPHAM.

Protestantism, etc.

1.

My dear young Friends,—I have something to say to you which will probably be a surprise, and I hope also a warning. Doubtless we are living in perilous times. " Now the Spirit speaketh expressly, that in the latter times some shall depart from the faith, giving heed to

seducing spirits, and doctrines of devils; speaking lies
in hypocrisy; having their conscience seared with a hot
iron; forbidding to marry, and commanding to abstain
from meats, which God hath created to be received
with thanksgiving of them which believe and know the
truth " (1 Tim. iv. 1—3). To so solemn a scripture
it becomes every Protestant to take heed. We may
indeed fear that few of us have truly valued our Protestant mercies and privileges. They deserve to be
held as a great gift of God to this nation. We have
long *enjoyed* them without realising their greatness and
their source; and we are sleeping in the security we
imagine to be our inalienable, unlosable birthright. Our
dependence on God, for a continuance of mercy, we forget. The *spirit* of the prayer, " Give us this day our
daily bread," seems far from us. But abuse of, unthankfulness for, our mercies may procure a removal of
them. The only inalienable blessings are in Christ, and
belong to His Church. Israel, after the flesh, has long
since lost all her national blessings, and so may England
lose her Protestantism. The Anglican Church which
was once regarded as a bulwark against Popery, it is
not possible so to regard to-day. And whoever thinks
that the national sentiment of freedom will help in the
time of trial will sadly prove that he trusted in the
" shadow of Egypt." But some of you may say, " Surely
our great Nonconformist bodies, Arminians though they
are, will stand for their privileges, and our national
freedom." Very likely you do not realise the deep
truth there is in the saying of Toplady: " Arminianism is the spawn of Popery." It is true. And here
comes in my surprise and warning to you. Recently,
two Protestant meetings were held in Brighton, and I
thought it my duty to attend them. They were held
to give a " startling exposure " of the work of a Catholic
bishop among Nonconformists. This bishop is known
as the " Bishop of Mercia and Middlesex," and it is said
that he is " the one man in England above all others
who is making the Romanising of the Free Churches
possible." At the meetings I attended it was said that

this bishop had ordained several Nonconformist ministers, who have a dispensation to continue in their pas-
torates and pose as Nonconformists. He has visited
Brighton, and has held a meeting in a Hall connected
with a Congregational chapel, and has tried to obtain a
church in which to ordain a Nonconformist minister.
All the above was stated in the meetings. Is it not
startling and alarming? So far as I know, there has
been no public contradiction made of any of the above
statements.

Now, you may be disposed to ask how it is possible
for men, professing the religion of the Bible, to forget
their profession so far as to stoop to so evil a thing.
Of course, it is done secretly. The bishop is reported to
have said to one to whom he gave an interview, " The
worst of it is these things have to be done clandes-
tinely." But grace puts an end to all the " unfruitful
works of darkness " where *it* reigns.

What, then, is the secret of the above threatening
proceedings? It is twofold. i. *The rejection of the
Word of God.* When a man rejects the inspiration of
the Scriptures, he rejects that by which " the man of
God may be perfect, throughly furnished unto all good
works " (2 Tim. iii. 17). Remember what the Lord
said by Jeremiah. Why were the stork, and the turtle,
and the crane, and the swallow wiser than the wise
men? *Because* the wise men rejected the Word of the
Lord (chap. viii. 7—9). They were foolish people, and
without understanding; they had eyes, and yet they saw
not; ears, and heard not. It is even so to-day. Men
may acquire extensive knowledge and yet possess not an
atom of wisdom. ii. *The lack of the Holy Ghost.* If
He be not the Teacher of a sinner, how can he know
anything of God or His glorious kingdom? " Except
a man be born of water and of the Spirit, he cannot
enter into the kingdom of God " (Jno. iii. 5). And if a
man be not in the kingdom of God he cannot walk in
the laws and ordinances of it, cannot seek its peace
and interests; he must seek the peace and interests of
the kingdom of darkness.

May this word of warning be made useful to you.
Be careful of all you hear. If any hint is dropped
about the Bible not being sufficient, or lacking authority; any commendation of ceremony; any soft word
about Popery, tending to remove from your minds its
abominations and lessen your loathing and horror of it,
God grant you may suspect and turn away from such
hint, and from him who utters it. May the Holy
Ghost teach you, and save you from the snare of the
fowler, and lead you, as utterly ruined and lost sinners,
to Christ, the only Saviour, Redeemer, and High Priest.
So prays,

Your affectionate friend,

Brighton, April, 1922.   J. K. Popham.

2.

My dear young Friends,—On January 16 a debate
took place in the Dome, Brighton, between "Father"
Bede Jarrett, O.F., Provincial of the English Domini-
cans, and the "Rev. W. A. Limbrick, F.R.Hist. Society
(Vicar of Epping Upland, and Secretary of the Protestant Reformation Society)." Subject: "The Open
Bible: Is it a blessing or a curse?" The Dome, which
seats 4,000, was full. I was invited by the Protestant
Organising Committee, and felt it my duty to attend. I
avoid all so-called evangelical meetings, but this meeting
seemed quite different in character. The question of
an open Bible appealed to me, though, knowing something of the history of Roman Catholicism, I feared
there might be some disturbance, but we had the advantage of an exceedingly able, strong, and fair Chairman,
A. O. Jennings, Esq., J.P., M.B.E., LL.B. The debate
arose out of a remark made on a Lord's day afternoon
on the beach at Brighton, by a Romish priest, "That
an open Bible was a curse." The bold and wicked
assertion was taken up by the Protestants of the town,
and the above meeting was the result. Rome sent one
of her ablest men, and Protestantism was not a whit
behind in sending the very able and redoubtable Vicar

of Epping Upland. On both sides the debate was con-
ducted with courtesy.

The Romanist opened the discussion; forty minutes
seemed not too long in which to elaborate and prove his
side of the question. And what line did he take? Did
he take the course his brother priest took on the beach?
No, he was too wise for that. He occupied a large pro-
portion of his time in telling us that the Bible is a
beautiful Book, divinely inspired, and therefore without
error. He was sure that all in that large gathering,
Protestants and Catholics alike, were agreed on that
point. He told us that we all, every one, loved God
intensely and desired to serve Him. All this was said
with the suavity, quiet emphasis, and polish of a gentle-
man, and an accomplished speaker, whose every word,
every syllable, was distinctly heard by that vast
assembly. He then approached the crucial question,
" Is this Bible," which he again praised, " when open, a
blessing or a curse? " Again he was gentle, walked
round the question. Of course, it was to be read. Every
Roman Catholic priest must read a portion of it every
day, and read it through once a year on pain of mortal
sin. Every Catholic boy learns it at school. But the
question must be argued. So at length we were told
it was not to be read indiscriminately, because all are
not competent to read it. That was, in substance, the
reason, the only reason given. No word about the curse,
about Rome's forbidding the reading of the Bible. If a
Romish Bishop gave his written consent, a Roman
Catholic might read it. The speech was a fine exhibi-
tion of Jesuitical chicanery. Jesuitism has been described as " designing, cunning, prevaricating." That
sinister art was shown to perfection.

Then came Mr. Limbrick's turn. He read a most
learned, able, and clear speech. It was entirely convin-
cing, but his delivery was too rapid to permit an
intelligent following. The Council of Trent, Popes'
Bulls, and edicts against reading and possessing the
Bible were read, and no doubt would be quite new to
many. But his time was too short. The abundant

object lessons which the contrasted histories and conditions of Protestant and Roman Catholic countries afford, could not be produced fully.

After the two main speeches, each speaker was allowed fifteen minutes for reply. To the Protestant champion, the priest could only say that his quotations from Councils, Popes' Bulls, etc., were not to the point. They were inconvenient, that was the point. Again, Mr. Limbrick would have the Bible and its blessings. Then the priest was given five minutes in which to wind up the debate. It was a memorable evening, and afforded much matter for reflection, and I thought you would be interested to hear about what is probably rather uncommon to-day. And also it occurred to me that we might usefully employ a little of our time together in considering for ourselves the important question: "Is the open Bible a blessing or a curse?"

i. *Let us regard the question from our own national view-point.* Has the open Bible been a blessing or a curse? None of you can doubt the answer. Our national liberties did not come from the Papal suppression of Bible reading, the burning of its anxious Spirit-taught readers, and of the divine Book itself. We all know that the God-given, blessed Reformation came from the reading and application of the Word of God, the incorruptible Word (Jas. i. 18; 1 Pet. i. 23). And men, born again, and their gifts and learning sanctified, gave the nation the Bible. By that, sinners were born again, received the Word as the very Word of God, and withdrew from the apostate Church of Rome, lest they should be partakers of her plagues, resisted her idolatrous claims, threw off her galling yoke, fled her pollutions, and procured our liberties. Our prosperity and our greatness among the nations of the earth are the result of an open Bible.

ii. *View the question from a church point.* Godly men saw that the Church of Rome was the "Mystery, Babylon the Great, the mother of harlots and abominations of the earth, the woman drunken with the blood of the saints, and with the blood of the martyrs of

Jesus. And they heard a voice from heaven saying, Come out of her, My people, that ye be not partakers of her sins, and that ye receive not of her plagues" (Rev. xvii. 5, 6; xviii. 4). And God founded visible churches, and sinners were converted unto Him, and they fled as doves to their windows, and the walls of Jerusalem were built. And what glory has redounded to God from the churches made free by divine grace and an open Bible!

iii. *Consider it from the personal view-point.* The child Timothy had no letter of priestly permission to read "the Holy Scriptures"; he read them with his mother. The twelve tribes which were scattered abroad were begotten with the Word of truth, each one personally (Jas. i. 18); they were led to desire the sincere milk of the Word (1 Pet. ii. 2). What blessed experience the Thessalonians had of the power of the Word as it came to them in the Holy Ghost (1 Thess. i. 5, 8). Idolatry, immorality, all manner of sin and open wickedness have been cast out by the Word of God brought to sinners. By reading the Word of God, from what mistakes, wrong paths, and flagrant evils have His people been saved (Ps. cxix. 9, 11, 29). With gracious power has the Spirit taken the Word and applied it to fearing hearts, to doubting souls, to perplexed ones, and each has found a blessing in it.

On the other hand, so far from the open Bible being a curse, the withholding of the sacred Volume is a greater sin than withholding corn. If he that withholdeth corn is cursed by the people (Prov. xi. 26), how much more shall God curse, punish, and plague the priest who withholds and burns His Word; yea, and who takes away from, or adds to it (Rev. xxii. 18, 19). The nation, the church, the household, the person that possesses the Bible, possesses that which is able to make wise unto salvation. For "all Scripture is given by inspiration of God, and is profitable for doctrine, for reproof, for correction, for instruction in righteousness: that the man of God may be perfect, throughly furnished unto all good works" (2 Tim. iii. 15—17).

Dear young friends, keep your Bibles, read them carefully and much; who knows whether the Holy Ghost, who moved holy men of old to write the Scriptures, will speak to you by them, and make you wise unto salvation.

Your affectionate friend,

Brighton, March, 1923.   J. K. POPHAM.

3.

My dear young Friends,—Of course you are acquainted with the word " Protestant," and, generally, of its meaning; but perhaps you have not given to it the consideration it deserves. The word is full of deep meaning. It is historical, political, and theological. It sharply divides nations. Roughly, it is a *Protest against Popery*. The word expresses powerful conviction which made men count not their lives dear unto them, carried them into exile, to prison, and the stake, suffering the loss of all things for Christ's sake. Out of it came Strict Baptists, who were often in early days called Ana-baptists; the Lutherans, Genevan, Anglican (Reformed), Puritan bodies, or denominations.

I said it is a *Protest against Popery;* for without doubt the Pope is an Anti-christ, " Who opposeth and exalteth himself above all that is called God, or that is worshipped; so that he as God sitteth in the temple of God, showing himself that he is God " (2 Thess. ii. 4). He blasphemes Christ by the idolatrous mass, in which he declares that he offers up in that pernicious service the divinity, blood, and bones of the Lord Jesus. He degrades the Lord of lords and King of kings by setting up His mother above Him, and she is invoked to intercede to move Him to be propitious. Popery denies the efficacy of Christ's vicarious death by adding human merit. It debases the Scripture by adding Popish decrees; it makes sin easy by indulgences; it makes heaven doubtful by the horrible invention of purgatory. It removes the simplicity and equality of the gospel ministry by the invention of pope, cardinal, priest, and a variety of orders. It has ever been a hot-bed of immorality, a cabal of intrigue against Protestant States. This apostate church is the mother of harlots, a violent, relentless persecutor of the saints of God, with whose blood she is drunk.

Now against this accursed system God's people *protest*. By divine grace they perceive the evil of the system, and that the Pope is undoubtedly an antichrist. Every approach to God the Father through God the Son, by the gracious operation of God the Spirit, is a secret, gracious protest of faith against the wicked intervention of the Popish religion. Every Protestant sermon on justification by the righteousness of Christ received by faith is a public repudiation of Popery. All holy living by the grace of Christ is a silent witness against the vile living which Popery has ever condoned. How Luther thundered against Popery!

But there are many antichrists in the world. He is antichrist that denieth the Father and the Son, for he contradicts the testimony of the Holy Ghost: " For there are Three that bear record in heaven, the Father, the Word, and the Holy Ghost: and these Three are One " (1 Jno. v. 7). May God give you grace to hate and protest against every voice that denies the Trinity, and salvation by the incarnate Son; grace to protest against all sin in every shape.

Against Communism raise a protest in every way open to you. For the root principle of that sinister system is the destruction of all religion. This terrible fact is not a secret which has leaked out and is known only to a few. It is the avowed principle of its leaders. And the English Communists must know it. May we all sigh and cry for that abomination which is in our land.

Against spiritism, familiar spirits, commerce with the dead, raise your voice.

Against Arminianism, " the spawn of Popery," as Toplady called it, lift up your voice. For it robs God of His sovereignty, Christ of His purchase, and the Spirit of His invincible work.

Against the fashion of this world lift the silent voice of nonconformity. Against the " shame " of the woman

who cuts off her hair which is given her for a covering
and glory, show your abhorrence.

May God bless you all with His love and mercy in
the washing of regeneration and renewing of the Holy
Ghost. For that will make you spiritual Protestants,
and they are the only Protestants who will withstand
in the evil day and having done all, will stand.

Your affectionate friend,

Brighton, August, 1926.   J. K. POPHAM.

4.

My dear young Friends,—If Protestantism be said
to be a negative, it must ever be maintained that it
protests against errors, affirming, in its turn, that those
errors are the negative of Scripture. It has therefore
a positive position. And true Protestants will ever be
raised up by God in His all-wise providence to affirm
that Popery is against God, and fights against the
Scriptures, that it is a blasphemy against Christ, an
unblushing defacing of His fairest form, the destruction
of His perfect work, the torment of its deluded followers
by subjugating the freedom, the manhood of conscience.
And this heavy indictment the Protestant is prepared to
maintain. I doubt not you all generally believe in that
which Popery denies. I say *generally*, for there is a
particular belief, by the grace of God. God grant each
of us the faith of His elect, that we may receive the
truth in love and hold it in righteousness. But our
denominational Protestantism, like the nation's, is an
inheritance worthy to be maintained at all costs.

We believe that only one God is to be worshipped:
"Hear, O Israel, the Lord our God is one Lord." But
Popery has made many gods, canonised innumerable
saints (so called), especially Mary, the mother of Jesus.
Justly all generations have called her blessed; for great
was the honour conferred on her to be the maiden
mother of the body prepared for the Son of God. But
that honour does not entitle her to the position in
heaven accorded to her by the Papists. Nowhere in the
Scripture of truth is found the Mariolatry of Popery.

To find it we have to go to apocryphal writings. That fact alone is sufficient warrant for every true Protestant to reject emphatically the worship of the mother of Jesus. Always turn away from every doctrine which is not revealed in the Word of God. Follow noble Luther in his reiteration, *the Bible, the Bible, the Bible.* Far otherwise must it ever be with the Romish priest. He *must* go to apocryphal writings. The *Protevangelium Jacobi* is said to be the real source of Mariolatry, the kernel of which may have been written in the second century, but which received its present shape two centuries later. But according to Ewald, a German writer—born 1704, died 1741—"the whole cultus of Mary in the Papal church rests upon the book, '*Transitus Mariæ*,' in which 'All created beings are incited to adore her.'" Thus you will see that Mariolatry may claim antiquity, but not Scripture. And what is not found in Holy Scripture, though it *claim* to be from heaven, must be rejected, if it teach what is contrary to the divine Word. Let us see, then, what the Church of Rome teaches with respect to the mother of Jesus. The Roman Breviary, reformed by order of the Council of Trent, and published by order of Pius V., revised by Popes Clement VII. and Urban VIII., translated by John, Marquis of Bute, frequently to be repeated, prays, "Holy Mary, Mother of God, pray for us sinners now at the hour of our death. O Holy Mary, be thou a help to the helpless, a strength to the fearful, a comfort to the sorrowful, pray for the people, plead for the clergy, make intercession for all women vowed to God; may all that keep thine holy remembrance feel the might of thine assistance. Pray for us, O holy mother of God." She is called "the mother of mercy," "our advocate," and is asked to show Jesus to her worshippers. Mary is addressed in a hymn as "Mercy seat of the world, the ladder which raises every one by grace." I have thus given you an epitome of Mariolatry, a part of the theology and worship of the apostate Church of Rome; a part, of which her eminent apologist, Cardinal Newman, writes: "I have said that there was in the first

ages no public and ecclesiastical recognition of the
place which St. Mary holds in the economy of grace;
this was reserved for the fifth century." So you see
Mariolatry is not *in* the Bible; her place in worship
was fixed about 500 years after the completion of the
Canon of the infallible and sufficient revelation of the
economy of salvation. Need Protestants any further
condemnation of Mariolatry? Who inspired fallible
men to add to God's Word in the fifth century what
they deem a cardinal doctrine? Fearful will it be for
them when they experience the word of the Holy Ghost:
" If any man shall add unto these things, God shall add
unto him the plagues which are written in this book ",
(Rev. xxii. 18).

Let us now see what God teaches with respect to
worship. " Thou shalt have no other gods before Me.
Thou shalt not make unto thee any graven image, or
any likeness of anything that is in heaven above or that
is in the earth beneath or that is in the water under
the earth. Thou shalt not bow down thyself to them,
nor serve them: for I, the Lord thy God, am a jealous
God, visiting the iniquities of the fathers upon the
children unto the third and fourth generation of them
that hate Me. And showing mercy unto thousands of
them that love Me, and keep My commandments "
(Exod. xx. 3—6). Idolatry became one of the chief sins
of Israel, one of the causes of their famines, defeats,
and captivities. The same awful, holy jealousy is
revealed in the Gospel. " Ye (Samaritans) worship ye
know not what: we know what we worship; for salvation is of the Jews. But the hour cometh, and now is,
when the true worshippers shall worship the Father in
spirit and in truth: for the Father seeketh such to
worship Him. God is a Spirit; and they that worship
Him must worship Him in spirit and in truth " (Jno. iv.
22—24). The Gospel in the power of the Holy Ghost
threw down the pagan dagons in the hearts of all who
were effectually called, so that Paul, writing to the
church at Corinth, could say: " For though there be
that are called gods, whether in heaven or in earth (as

there be gods many, and lords many); but to us there is but one God, the Father, of whom are all things, and we in Him; and one Lord Jesus Christ, by whom are all things, and we by Him " (1 Cor. viii. 5, 6). See also and read carefully Acts xiv. 13—17; xvii. 22—31; 1 Thess. i. 8, 10.

God grant you to see and feel His jealousy burning against idols and idolators, that you may flee from everything in you, and without, which would, Pope-like, sit in His rightful place, opposing Him, and exalting itself above all that is called God, and to be worshipped. *Honour* the virgin mother of Jesus, but *flee from and hate Mariolatry.*

Your affectionate friend,

Brighton, September, 1928.   J. K. POPHAM.

5.

My dear young Friends,—Having written a few words to you about one of the heresies of the Church of Rome, I feel disposed to take up another of them, which is worse than Mariolatry. For the doctrine of the Mass, the subject of this letter, appears to me to surpass all the other evils of that apostate Church. If the undue, unscriptural honour given to Mary, dishonours Christ, what can be said of the Mass, which denies the efficacy of His vicarious sacrifice of Himself? Oh, that we all knew Christ and loved Him, so as to unite with the Psalmist in protesting to God: " Do not I hate them, O Lord, that hate Thee? and am not I grieved with those that rise up against Thee? I hate them with perfect hatred: I count them mine enemies " (Ps. cxxxix. 21, 22). I know that the religious world disapproves of what are called the imprecatory Psalms, but let it be enough for us to believe that every word of God is pure, that God is the everlasting God, and His glorious character more important than whole worlds.

That we may have an accurate knowledge of what the Mass is, let us turn to " The Service of the Mass in the Greek and Roman Churches," by the Rev. C. H. H.

Wright, D.D., Religious Tract Society: "The Mass: A rite whereby it is supposed that Christ in the integrity of His Person, human and divine, in or under the form of a wheaten cake and a cup of wine, is sacrificed by a priest, as a propitiation of God and in expiation of sin. This doctrine was not officially imposed till the sixteenth century, at the Council of Trent, but it is a natural consequence from the doctrine of Transubstantiation sanctioned in the thirteenth century, and from the un-scientific form of the latter doctrine, known as the objective Presence in the elements held by some who are unaware of the consequences involved in it. That the wheaten cake and cup of wine become Christ on the pronunciation of a formula by the priest, belongs primarily to the doctrine of Transubstantiation. That after having been thus brought upon the altar, He is first offered and then sacrificed, by the priest, is the specific doctrine of the Sacrifice of the Mass." To meet the objection against this doctrine, that a sacrifice means the destruction of that which is sacrificed, the Romish theologians had recourse to horrible subtleties. Bellar-mine, "the Doctor or Teacher of the Latin Church, whose dicta none may question," asks, "In what con-sists the essence of the Sacrifice of the Mass?" Four opinions, he replies, are tenable. "(1) It consists in the eating and drinking of the priest, because by that takes place the destruction of the victim. (2) It con-sists in the oblation or offering of Christ by the priest. (3) It consists in the consecration alone, because in it the oblation is included, and also there is a destruction of the victim, because by force of the words of consecra-tion the body of Christ is at the moment separated from the blood, and this causes His death. (4) It consists partly in the consecration, partly in the priests' eating and drinking; the consecration placing the victim on the altar, and the priests' eating and drinking con-suming it. For a true and real sacrifice requires a true and real destruction of the thing offered, but this does not take place except by the priests' eating and drink-ing by which the sacramental essence of Christ is destroyed. A sacrament is not completed without a true and real destruction. For the sacrifice to be effected on the altar, it is necessary that first the victim be placed upon it in its integrity, and then that it be destroyed." Thus far the doctrine of the Mass. One says, "We cannot wonder at Dean Field, after stating the authorised Roman doctrine, bursting out with indignation, 'But it is impious to think of destroying Christ in any sort.'" Impious indeed! The doctrine of the Mass is a doctrine of devils. May we all abhor such a doctrine. But this is a doctrine of the Church with which in some form and measure the Archbishops, bishops, and thousands of ministers in the Church of England desire to be in union. And yet, from the Archbishop of Canterbury down to the curate, each one subscribes to the "Articles of Religion," of which the thirty-first is: "The offering of Christ once made is that perfect redemption, propitiation, and satisfaction, for all the sins of the whole world, both original and actual; and there is none other satisfaction for sin, but that alone. Wherefore the sacrifice of masses in the which it was commonly said, that the priest did offer Christ for the quick and the dead, to have remission of pain or guilt, were blasphemous fables, and dangerous deceits." It were surely enough that such blasphemous fables and dangerous deceits should be taught in the Church of Rome by thousands of priests in our nation, but it is the essence of iniquity that men ordained as ministers in the National Protestant Church, who vowed to do their utmost to banish from the realm Popish doctrines, and who eat Protestant bread, should do their utmost to undermine and pull down the house which wise and godly men built. Oh, but when God arises to judge such men as thus disregard and break their pledges, He will say, "Hear the Word of the Lord, ye rulers of Sodom; give ear unto the law of our God, ye people of Gomorrah," etc. (Isa. i. 10—15). The Mass of the Ritualist is not an acceptable sacrifice, but a vain oblation; his incense an abomination; his new moons and appointed feasts the holy God hates; his spreading forth his hands is not regarded by the Lord, and his many prayers are not heard.

I conclude this letter with an expression of fervent desire that the God of all grace may so convince you of your sins, original and actual, as that your consciences may never rest till comforted by the blood of sprinkling which speaketh better things than that of Abel; in that blessed case you will reject, hate, and abhor the doctrine of devils—the Mass.

Your affectionate friend,

Brighton, October, 1928.   J. K. POPHAM.

6.

My dear young Friends,—Out of my last to you on the blasphemous fable and deceit of the Romish Mass there may have grown in your minds an anticipation of a word on the related subject, the priest. A sacrifice must needs have a sacrificer.

We will begin then with the Word of God on this solemn and vitally important subject. In the sacred Volume there are three priesthoods set forth. i. The Aaronic. Aaron the Levite, the brother of Moses, was called to the honour of being the priest. He and his sons stood in that office until the end of the typical dispensation. One essential element in priesthood is mediation. "For every high priest taken from among men is ordained for men in things pertaining to God, that he may offer both gifts and sacrifices for sins: who can have compassion on the ignorant, and on them that are out of the way; for that he himself is compassed with infirmity" (Heb. v. 1, 2). The purity, the wellbeing of the elect nation hung on the due observance of the divine commandment respecting the worship of God, and worship was by sacrifices. The Divine Majesty was served by the people through the priest, who offered the commanded sacrifices. But, while the covenanted nation was righteous, clean, and prosperous so long as it brought the daily offerings and the yearly atonement, as He Himself said by Azariah, the son of Oded, "Hear ye me, Asa, and all Judah, and Benjamin: the Lord is with you while ye be with Him; and if ye seek Him, He will be found of you; but if ye forsake Him, He will forsake you" (2 Chron. xv. 2); yet both the nation and the priesthood were typical, a shadow of good things to come (Heb. x. 1). The law made nothing perfect. The priestly offerings never purified a conscience, and so never gave true satisfaction either to God or man. And because the whole dispensation was not an end in itself but only a type, it was not introduced or confirmed by an oath. When, therefore, the ever-gracious and glorious Anti-type came, the Levitical priest, as a priest, died. He was no longer needed.

ii. The second High Priest came. Christ was called of God, who said to Him: "Thou art a Priest for ever after the order of Melchisedec" (Heb. v. 6). He is a Priest for ever: "But this Man, because He continueth ever, hath an unchangeable Priesthood" (Heb. vii. 24), His Priesthood cannot pass to another. In this, and in other vital points, He differs from the Levitical priest: "And they truly were many priests, because they were not suffered to continue by reason of death." As the Son of God is our Great High Priest there cannot be another High Priest, for God has only one Son: "But last of all, He sent His Son." He alone, incarnate, is capable of being the Mediator of the better covenant, and of making an end of sin by the sacrifice of Himself. For by one offering He hath perfected for ever them that are sanctified. Therefore, in the covenant of grace, God says, "And their sins and iniquities will I remember no more. Now where remission of these is, there is no more offering for sin" (Heb. x. 14, 18). By this Priest a searched, divided creature, who realises that all his inward things are naked and opened unto the eyes of Him with whom he has to do, approaches—comes boldly—"unto the throne of grace to obtain mercy, and find grace to help in time of need" (Heb. iv. 12—16). Thus, while the law made nothing perfect, the bringing in of a better hope did; by the which we draw nigh unto God, even by our Great High Priest.

iii. The priest is the believer (Rev. i. 6; 1 Pet. ii. 9;
Heb. xiii. 15). This priesthood belongs to the Church
of God. The offering up of the Gentiles is acceptable,
being sanctified by the Holy Ghost. When a poor
sinner sees the new and living Way, and by faith enters,
and approaches God therein, bringing his poor, broken,
bruised heart by Jesus Christ, he is accepted in the
Beloved, and his praises are melody both in his heart
and in heaven.

Where, then, is the priest of the apostate Church of
Rome, and, I may add, the Anglo-Catholic ? Not in the
heavenly places in Christ. He is in darkness, heresy,
death and condemnation. He blasphemes, degrades,
dispossesses the only Priest—Christ Jesus. He deludes
poor people; he offends the Majesty of heaven; while to
all true children of God he is a deceiver and an Anti-
christ. Flee, dear young people, from all pretending
priests. God give you to feel your need of our Great
High Priest, and grant you a *felt* interest in Him.

Your affectionate friend,

Brighton, November, 1928.   J. K. POPHAM.

7.

My dear young Friends,—Doubtless you will have
read and heard much about the Deposited Book, and
the rejection of it by the House of Commons after the
surprising vote in its favour by the House of Lords.
Its rejection was like a miracle, and no doubt an answer
to prayer. For a time the Protestant character of
England is preserved. For this so unexpected a deliverance praises have gone up to the Lord of hosts from
many hearts that were sad and grieved at the prospect
of becoming part of Papal Rome. For notwithstanding
the smooth assurances of the authors of the changed book,
that would have been the result of its passing and being
signed by the King. Nor ought we now to rest in the
present state of things. The quiet acquiescence in
exercise of its undoubted right by the House of Commons, the proclaimed intention to remove ambiguities,
which, it was assumed, caused its rejection—ambiguities,

please observe, not the Romish doctrines which are not ambiguous, but obvious—the reference which is to be made to the House of Convocation, are signs which it would be folly to ignore. We should be on our guard. May we still pray that the attempt to hand this nation over to Rome may never succeed. The enemy will not relax his efforts. Rest not in the adverse vote, wonderful, miraculous though it was. Put not confidence in any man. Two things I would put before you with respect to the danger which I think will reappear. i. *Remember the Lord of hosts.* If true Protestants are comparatively few in the land—there were only about seven thousand in Israel in Elijah's time—if the few are enabled to wait on God, and seek His intervention, who knoweth if He will again frustrate the designs of the enemies of the cross of Christ? King Jehoshaphat found assurance, comfort, and deliverance in calling on God in heaven (2 Chron. xx.). Gideon's three hundred men with pitchers and lamps within, and the all-victorious cry, " The sword of the Lord, and of Gideon," found success. The authority and power of God over Nebuchadnezzar and his furnace, over the presidents and princes of Darius, and the lions, we should do well to remember. Also we should ponder the question which spreads itself over the whole world of difficulties and seeming impossibilities: " Is there anything too hard for the Lord? " ii. *If opportunity is given you to speak and contend for the Protestant character of our beloved nation, embrace it.* Do all you can, say all you can to maintain that which has been our honour and glory in the world. Oh, to be jealous of, and zealous for, your birthright! For what would our becoming a Popish nation mean? i. It would mean that our greatest possession, the inspired Bible, if not snatched from our hands, would be preached up as a Book beyond us, we should be told that we laymen are not competent to understand it, and therefore must not be permitted to read it without permission from a priest or bishop. Think of it. The Bible, God's holy and infallible Book, for the translating of which Tyndale was martyred, put under lock and key! Have any of you noticed in the speeches of the Archbishops and bishops, and all the advocates of the Deposited Book, the omission of all reference to the Word of God? The one word in all the speeches and letters was the Church. The Church, no longer intended to be the church of Cranmer, Hooper, Ridley, Latimer, Bradford, and others, but of Rome, without, for the moment, the Pope. ii. It would mean that the Mass would be legalised. Now, many, who violate their ordination vows, are permitted by their bishops to practise that blasphemous thing, dishonouring, degrading the Person and efficacious work of our only adorable Lord and Saviour, Jesus Christ. Now, with the Popish Book rejected, the children of God must go before the Lord, and with Daniel say, " O Lord, to us belongeth confusion of face, to our kings, our princes, and to our fathers, because we have sinned against Thee." But if what is now done *against law* should become *lawful*, if we cast behind our back the blessed God-given Reformation, what could we say before the Lord?

The first Bishop of Liverpool was J. C. Ryle. He was a Protestant, and wrote largely. One small work of his is, " The Reign of James II. and the Trial of the Seven Bishops." It is issued by C. J. Farncombe and Sons, Ltd., price 6d. I advise you to get it, and *read* it. You will then see England's *second deliverance from Romanism.* May God grant that the future historian may write of the important and wonderful vote of the House of Commons on December 15th, 1927, that it was *the third deliverance of England from Romanism.*

And may eternal life, and so, eternal deliverance from sin, be given to you. Thus prays,

Your affectionate friend,

Brighton, February, 1928.   J. K. POPHAM.

P.S.—Having the proof of my monthly letter before me, I feel disposed to add a word about a remarkable providence in connection with the work of the Archbishops and bishops in attempting to so frame the rejected Deposited Book as to get it through Parliament. I refer to the "crushing Encyclical" of the Pope, and the publication by Lord Halifax of his "Notes on the Conversations at Malines, 1921—1925," in "defiance of the expressed wish of the Archbishop of Canterbury," *Morning Post,* Thursday, January 12th, 1928. Well might the above paper head its notes: "Bishops' new trouble," and "Complications." And if, as is reported, Lord Halifax has recently had an audience with the Pope, the simultaneous appearance of the Conversations and the Encyclical is much to be observed. Let us watch. The Lord sitteth King for ever. The consternation of the bishops can be imagined, and the change which the revelations may work in many Evangelicals may possibly be designed by the divine Majesty for good to this nation.

8.

My dear young Friends,—The recent decision of Parliament not to legalise Popish doctrines in the National Church ought to be much and thankfully observed by us all. Not to be thankful for so signal a mercy would be to sin against God, from whom it came, and to be in the solemn and condemnatory words of Holy Scripture: "Because that, when they knew God (in the revelation of His otherwise invisible things), they glorified Him not as God, neither were they thankful;" and, "They remembered not His hand, nor the day when He delivered them from the enemy" (Rom. i. 21; Ps. lxxviii. 42). Unthankfulness and forgetfulness are grievous sins. They are so counted among men. How much more with respect to Him in whom we live and move and have our being, and from whom comes our well-being. For the second time the Protestantism of our beloved nation has been challenged, and by divine mercy the answer has been unequivocally given. Of course, the Anglo-Catholics will continue in their sin and illegalities. But for a body of men to violate the law of the Church in whose doctrines they avowed their belief when they were admitted into her ministry, is one thing;

it would be another and more terrible thing for Parliament to legalise the sin, yea, the double sin of violating their ordination vows, and going in the face of the distinct teaching of Holy Scripture.

While giving unto the Lord the glory due unto His Name (Ps. xxix. 2), let us not forget that the enemy of Protestantism, our highest national honour, will be working Romeward. Therefore, may we be enabled to pray that the Lord who mercifully gave us the blessed Reformation may be pleased to preserve to us that inestimable gift. But we shall be told that Protestantism is a negative, and therefore not a Faith. To one who does not think, this statement may appear true. But it is not so. We protest against the doctrine of the Mass because we receive and hold that Christ is our only Priest, and His complete obedience and one offering of Himself, our only perfection. Read Heb. x. We not only deny, *we affirm*. If therefore any of you should be assailed with the argument that Protestantism is a negation and not a Faith, be not shaken. Meet the statement with the direct, positive, powerful, and infallible statements of Holy Scripture. Produce chapter and verse to prove that Jesus Christ was called by His eternal Father to be a Priest for ever after the order of Melchisedec, and that He made an offering of Himself to God, and so perfected for ever them that are sanctified (Heb. x. 10—14). A Protestant may be, and should be, always affirming. He should fearlessly affirm that the death of Christ is the centre and circumference of the forgiveness of sin and the justification of sinners; affirm that the doctrine of the Mass is a "blasphemous deceit"; that it is an offence to God, and a degrading, grievous insult to the Lord Jesus; affirm, too, that the Protestant Faith lays in the dust as a corrupt, corrupting, and dead thing the sacrifice of the Mass, and the sacrificing priest.

The nation owes much, under the Lord God omnipotent, to our Home Secretary and the Attorney General,*

* Sir Wm. Joynson-Hicks (afterward Lord Brentford), and Sir Thos. Inskip.

for their bold, uncompromising opposition to the "Deposited Book" on both occasions of its appearance in the House of Commons. The gratitude of Protestants to them is deep, though necessarily unspoken.

I must express the wish of my heart that all of you may be, by the grace of God, more than militant Protestants, even that the grace of the Lord Jesus may be exceeding abundant in you with faith and love which is in Christ Jesus (1 Tim. i. 14).

Your affectionate friend,
Brighton, August, 1928.   J. K. POPHAM.

9.

My dear young Friends,—We will have for a text Exodus xii. 21—27 and Joshua iv. 1—7. Read these verses carefully that you may get into your minds the circumstances they relate and the reasons for the divine injunctions with regard to the future generations of Israel. The Passover was to be had in perpetual remembrance till a greater Passover superseded it. Deliverance from Egypt was the beginning of the life of Israel, the fulfilling to them of the promise of God to their father Abraham (Gen. xii. 7). Joshua iv. 1—7 tells of the passing of Israel over Jordan as by dry land. My object in noting the above scriptures is to say to you that there are events in the life and history of England which we all should ever keep in grateful memory, events so great and so interwoven no one can forget them as history, but the significance, the influence, and their relation to our future are differently regarded by very different parties.

But first, let us briefly view some events we ought ever to remember and tell our children. *The blessed Reformation should never be forgotten.* By that mighty work of God England was delivered from the darkness, pollution, and blasphemies of Popery, the Bible was translated and opened, and people eagerly read it and the gospel had great success. This wonder of God is differently viewed to-day by many people. The Papists have always denounced and cursed it. But now many in the National Church, Anglo-Catholics (beginning with the Archbishops, bishops and thousands of clergymen) regard the Reformation as evil, and are doing their utmost to remove it. There is very little official Protestantism remaining to us. Now remember God's goodness to our nation in giving us the unspeakable blessing of an open Bible. If you are asked why you think so much of that Book tell your questioner it has wrought wonders in the land, that we owe, under God, all the greatness we have had among the nations and in the eyes of the world to the pure and purifying Word of God. Tell him that the liberties we enjoy to-day are the result of the reading of the inerrant Scriptures; that the preaching of the gospel, the writings of the Reformers, and later of the Puritans, the effectual calling of sinners by the Holy Ghost, the gathering of saints into visible churches, and the glory of God in and by such churches, all flow from the blessed Word of God in the hands of the good Spirit of God. These blessings are likely to be forgotten by us. But they were a real and mighty work of God in our land, and should be as a cherished memory, and jealously regarded as the memorial which the Israelites were commanded to keep. A youthful Israelite might say to his father, as he observed the care with which he was preparing the Passover, removing leaven from his house and attending to all the divine injunctions with respect to the solemnity, "Why do you make these preparations, what does the Passover mean?" Then his father was instructed to say, "It is the sacrifice of the Lord's Passover, who passed over the houses of the children of Israel in Egypt, when He smote the Egyptians, and delivered our houses."

You, dear young people, read the Bible, and I hope you believe it to have been given us by the inspiration of God. When (as, alas! is all too likely to be the case) you meet with opposers and questioners as to why you abstain from some things which they regard as proper such as the cinema, card playing, Sabbath-breaking, or why you do not read novels and the terrible trash which

is poured forth day by day, and why you attend chapel
with your parents, tell them the Bible forbids such sins,
and all sin. Say you are Protestants and admire
Protestant doctrine and practice, the Protestantism
which the Reformation gave to us. Be careful of this
ancient landmark. Once England *formally* repudiates
that, her sun will set. Indeed, we now so sadly disregard
the blessing, that we have reason to fear God is about
to reverse the order which has so long been our position
among the nations of the world. He *may* make us the
tail and not the head, the borrower and not the lender.
The Bible sets forth the glorious character of God, His
sovereign purposes with regard to all men, His redemption of His people by the Lord Jesus Christ, the
regenerating of them by the Holy Ghost, the glory of
the saints, the endless woe of the wicked. The Bible is
the grand centre of all revealed truth and goodness and
liberty; thence, as from a fountain, flow privileges and
mercies in the nation, in families, in churches. This
Book must always be the start and the finish with us.
From that, as from a fountain, have flowed the streams
of goodness which have made us glad. May we partake
of those streams by the mercy of the Holy Ghost.

Your affectionate friend,

Brighton, July, 1929. J. K. POPHAM.

National Outlook, etc.

1.

My dear young Friends,—How quickly the months
pass away, and how often I seem to be writing to you!
If apology were needed, it would be my interest in you
and my desire for your welfare. Your life is full of
difficulties. It will be all but impossible for you to
escape entirely the influence of the spirit of the times.
Where it is not as a storm, rooting up old customs,
carrying away many honoured traditions, it is a subtle
atmosphere insinuating itself into everything. No place,
no sphere of life, is free from it. Home, school, work-

shop, ideas of honour, views of contract, all places and things are invaded by this evil.

It may be asked if the change which has come to our beloved land can be rationally accounted for. I believe it can. i. There is a *cause* for it. ii. It may be re-regarded as an *effect*. i. There is a *cause* for it. The cause is *the rejection of the Word of God*. Read the calamities of the Jews as set forth in Jeremiah viii.; and if you ask *why* such terrible judgments, turn to the 9th verse. That explains all. And has not England rejected the God-given treasure of the Bible? We have chosen our own way, and there is no wisdom in us. ii. The troubles now in our midst may be regarded as an *effect*. When men, when nations, vex the Almighty, He turns to be their enemy. "Shall not My soul be avenged on such a nation as this?" He chooses His own weapons. "I will choose their delusions." None can properly doubt that He is punishing us. May He, in the midst of wrath, remember mercy!

One word of advice I venture to offer you, my young friends. Keep close to those who fear God; listen to them with respect to the Word of God. Avoid the intoxication of present-day teaching with respect to the removing of ancient landmarks. The Lord help you to revere His sacred Word, help you to seek His favour, teaching, and salvation, and the security which His children enjoy in Him. "Benjamin, the beloved of the Lord, shall dwell in safety by Him; and the Lord shall cover him all the day long, and he shall dwell between His shoulders."

Your affectionate friend,

Brighton, September, 1919.   J. K. POPHAM.

2.

My dear young Friends,—While wondering what to say to you this month, it came into my mind to say a few words on *thankfulness*. It is an inviting subject to a heart that is impressed with a sense of indebtedness to God. When men know not God, they do not glorify Him, neither are they thankful; but become vain in their imagination, and their foolish hearts are darkened (Rom. i. 21). May you, my readers, be saved from so sad, so condemned a condition.

We should be profoundly thankful. i. Because "we live, and move, and have our being in Him," who made us in His own image. How little do we realise this all-permeating fact! So little, therefore, do we thank God for our being. Our physical and mental powers, and their continuance, come from our only Preserver. Job, in his great affliction and sorrow, was enabled to regard the Lord as the Preserver of men (Job vii. 20). The mysterious and wonderful organisation of our body; its power for work; its long continuance in order; the divine provision for its hourly recurring needs; our mental capacity and power; the pleasure of acquiring knowledge, and the useful employment of acquired knowledge; the gift of speech and the pleasure of conversation; health and home; friends and their confidence and communion; all these, together with the untold, unnumbered delights of nature, opened to us in each season, we owe to the beneficence of our Creator and Preserver.

ii. It is no small mercy that we live in this our beloved Island. How God has favoured England! The good laws, hitherto so well, so justly administered; the liberty of person and press; the security of property; the sanctity of home; all these blessings we enjoy beyond most, if not all, other nations. But above all else, the Reformation (the foundation and strength of the above-mentioned blessings), the gift of the blessed Bible, and of a wonderful race of ministers, whose ministry God signally owned, and whose works are an inestimable good in the church, call for the liveliest praise.

iii. The ending of the war, and the return of most of our dear young men, who were brought safely through the terrible ordeal, is another cause for thankfulness; doubtless many of you have fathers, husbands, brothers, about whom you feared through those anxious months and years, and now, with mournful exceptions, you rejoice in their return. What cause for gratitude!

May not such mercies be passed by without special thanksgiving.

Perhaps this train of thought was induced by the, to me, pleasing fact, that recently there was a special meeting held at our chapel for thanksgiving for the safe return to their homes, and to us, of those survivors of our young men who went to the war. It was a pleasant sight to see them in the meeting. One member who gave thanks, thanked God for preserving the minds of wives and mothers, whose anxious cares had been so keen and pressing. I was struck with it, and pass it on to you; it may touch some. May God, in His infinite love, be pleased to bless you with spiritual blessings in Christ, that you may, above all other thanks, thank Him for eternal life, justification, sanctification, and everlasting consolation and good hope through grace.

Your affectionate friend,

October, 1919.   J. K. POPHAM.

3.

My dear young Friends,—How fresh in your memories will be the terrible earthquake which recently overthrew much of Japan. Who did not feel an indefinable sense of an inconceivably terrific force contained in the earth, locked up, unheard, unseen, impalpable, but capable of bursting forth in volcanic countries? Also who could avoid a deep sense of man's utter helplessness in the presence of such a foe, whenever its dormant force should be let loose and exert itself? In the solemn instance before us, a city, towns and villages, teeming with life one moment, the next moment, reeling, falling houses, great buildings, all tumbling into ruin and inextricable confusion, engulfing the horror-stricken people; while docks and ships were tossed by the boiling, raging sea as so much shingle, all heaved up by an unseen hand. Some of us will never forget our first sensations on reading of the perhaps unparalleled cataclysm.

From this solemn providence we may draw one or

two lessons which, with God's blessing, may be useful to us.

i. *Sin calls for judgment, whether personal or national*. Japan is an idolatrous nation, and none can properly doubt that the anger of God was in the fearful earthquake which destroyed so many lives, so much property, and especially perhaps, to many, the damage done to the "holy mountain" of the nation. God is to be known by the judgment which He executeth. He is God alone, and none else; He knows not any. All Dagons must fall before Him. Some may say, "But were the Japanese sinners above all others?" The answer is twofold: i. No. But sometimes the anger and judgment of God falls on some to set them as warnings to others (1 Cor. x. 11). ii. "Nay: but, except ye repent, ye shall all likewise perish" (Luke xiii. 1—3). In some way, at some time, judgment will overtake all ungodly nations. And because we English people have had the Word of God, the ministry of the gospel and the ordinances of Christ, above all other nations, our punishment will be the greater.

Earthquakes are, in Scripture, generally an evidence, or an outpouring of divine wrath. They may be physical, or they may be moral. Of the first sort, one is recorded in 1 Kings xix. 11; another, in Matt. xxvii. 51, as if the wrath of God against sin, which rent the holy soul of the Lord of life, the sin-Bearer, was reflected in the convulsion of nature. Who can stand when once He is angry? Of the second sort we read in Revelation: "And the seventh angel poured out his vial into the air; and there came a great voice out of the temple of heaven, from the throne, saying, It is done. And there were voices, and thunders, and lightnings; and there was a great earthquake, such as was not since men were upon the earth, so mighty an earthquake, and so great" (ch. xvi. 17, 18). Here powers, civil and ecclesiastical, may be intended; and fearful and widespread will be the upheaval, involving the church of God, not in the ruin, but in much sifting and suffering.

Let no one take refuge in the possible natural fact that we live in a country that is not liable to such fearful catastrophes as earthquakes, because apparently we do not, as it were, stand over fires ever ready to burst forth and spread death and destruction around us. Apart from the fact that earthquakes have occurred in our much-loved Island, one would ask, has God no other means or agents wherewith to punish a people, a nation, steeped in sin as we are? Fire and hail, the windows of heaven are opened and closed by His own hand. Rain is sent for mercy or correction. He will not again drown the world, but fervent heat will dissolve it; and might it not do so in a measure any day? Moreover, may not a moral, a civil earthquake occur, and overturn, and throw into utter confusion all our cherished order and privileges, the throne, and every valued thing? Are there no signs of such an upheaval, no rumblings? O, may we not be highminded, but fear! for nationally we are daily provoking the most High God.

ii. *The only hope for this sinning nation is national repentance,* a return to the verbally, plenarily inspired Bible, from which the Higher Critic (O woe be to him!) has done so much to turn us away. God give us to fear Him in all His judgments and manifestations of His anger. When the ungodly are scorched with the great heat of some judgment, they blaspheme His name, who hath power over such judgment; and they repent not to give Him glory (Rev. xvi. 9).

May mercy come to us in the midst of wrath. May it be given to us to believe that God is not mocked, that whatsoever a man sows that shall he also reap; and may "repentance toward God, and faith toward our Lord Jesus Christ" be wrought in us by the Holy Ghost. If such grace, mercy, and love come to us, what monuments of sovereign goodness we shall be!

Believe me, my dear readers,

Your affectionate friend and well-wisher,

Brighton, November, 1923. J. K. POPHAM.

4.

My dear young Friends,—God's mercy to our beloved country is much in my thoughts just now, and I am therefore writing a few words to you on this very important subject. Holy Scripture tells us that He is the "King of nations." And Christ, who is God, says, "By Me kings reign and princes decree justice. By Me princes rule, and nobles, even all the judges of the earth" (Prov. viii. 15, 16). And the Holy Ghost, by Paul, tells us that the Son of God upholds the worlds. He made them, and it is His prerogative to uphold, that is, rule over them, guide them, and see that they fulfil His purposes in making them. How little we think of this divine superintendence when we read of the affairs of the nations of the world.

Sparrows fly or fall just as He wills. How much more, men, statesmen, rulers, "powers that be, angels, and authorities, and powers," must be under the King of kings and Lord of lords. And though the confusion we see everywhere, violence, oppression, gambling, and now one of the worst of all known evils, Communism, make it difficult for all but the true believer in God to believe that order and good can be evolved out of the seething evils, yet Christ, who is the blessed and only Potentate, the King of kings and Lord of lords, shall show, in His time, things which, when seen in the light of Christ, will appear not only right, but wonderful in their fitting each into the other, and their ultimate setting—the glory of Him who worketh all things after the counsel of His own will.

Now with regard to our own nation, who can doubt the wonderful, merciful working of God in the timely discovery of the plots of Communists against peace, order, and good government? And probably if all could be told us which is well known, we should be filled with amazement at the kindness, wisdom, and power of God in our protection, preservation and good.

The inhuman aim of Communism is the overthrow of all moral good, carrying with it the destruction of material prosperity. It begins with terrible Atheism. In the "Times" of December 29, it is said that Zinovieff—a name too well known in England—has "issued an anti-religious appeal," in which he said (I hardly like to write the shameful words), "We will grapple with the Lord God in due season. We will vanquish Him in His highest heaven, and wherever He seeks refuge we shall subdue Him for ever." This unspeakable blasphemy makes one shudder. What does it lead to? "A Bolshevist war on religion." And the young are being taught that there is no God. The Communists—only another name for the same enemies of God and man—have many schools in this country and in France. In the latter country, according to the "Daily Mail" of January 2, it is reported that a "boy of 12 presides at a congress." A congress of child Bolsheviks was recently held at the Paris headquarters of the Communist party, and was presided over by a boy of 12! At this congress "Resolutions were adopted by which the children pledged themselves to do their utmost to avoid singing patriotic hymns, . . . to decline to raise their caps to the head-master and other teachers, and to denounce capitalistic principles and history." Now if such meetings are not publicly held to-day in our own beloved country, it is because God has recently exposed Zinovieff and his party. But there is no change in the men or their devilish principles. And how far they may be working in secret God knows perfectly, and it is to be hoped our Government has some information.

If any of you should meet with a youth who by suggestion or a word shows disrespect to our king and the institutions of the realm, and good laws and order, part company with him at once. Never forget Romans xiii. 1—10.

How can we be sufficiently thankful to God for His goodness to England? Value your birthright, and seek by all means to maintain it. Read the Word of God, listen to the preaching of the truth; read the history of our dear fatherland, of the Reformation;

follow good men; cleave to Protestantism, and seek to
fear the "King of nations" (Jer. x. 7). With, and
above all this, may the everlasting goodness, wisdom,
and power of God bring you into the citizenship of the
commonwealth of spiritual Israel (Eph. ii. 12).

Your affectionate friend,

Brighton, February, 1925.   J. K. POPHAM.

Mortality.

My dear young Friends,—I am reminded of the rapid
passage of time by the fact that shortly you will be
looking for the "Friendly Companion" for August.
And this reminder brings before me Watts' fine words:

"Time! what an empty vapour 'tis!
And days how swift they are!
Swift as an Indian arrow flies,
Or like a shooting star."

Whoever desires to banish this from his thoughts is
therein very unwise and ungracious; he has a spirit
vastly different from that of the Psalmist, who prayed,
"So teach us to number our days, that we may apply
our hearts unto wisdom" (Ps. xc. 12). It is well to
consider the *cause* of the mortality of our bodies. Of
this the Scriptures tell us definitely, "Wherefore as by
one man sin entered into the world, and death by sin:
and so death passed upon all men, for that all have
sinned" (Rom. v. 12). Death, then, is the result of sin,
it is sin-procured. Properly, therefore, it is a part of
the curse (Gen. ii. 7). This view of death invests it
with an awfulness unspeakable. In itself it is no relief,
no good, no blessing. Good men have deplored its
approach. "O spare me, that I may recover strength,
before I go hence, and be no more" (Ps. xxxix. 13).
"I said, O my God, take me not away in the midst of
my days" (Ps. cii. 24). Hezekiah wept sore when told
to set his house in order, because he must die, and not
live; to be deprived of the residue of his years was a
great evil in his eyes. Beautiful and pathetic is his

language in those solemn hours: "Mine age is departed,
and is removed from me as a shepherd's tent: I have cut
off like a weaver my life: He will cut me off with pining
sickness: from day even to night wilt Thou make an
end of me" (Isa. xxxviii. 12). To Job, in his affliction,
life was as wind. The Holy Ghost, by the apostle
James, tells us that our life is a vapour, which appeareth
for a little time, and then vanisheth away. The Bible
account and reckoning of life must ever be repulsive to
the mind of man. And indeed, it is an evil; evil in its
origin—sin; evil in its effect; it deprives us of tangible
pleasure, and of our chief desire—*present* good. But
worse than all else is the afterwards—" after death the
judgment."

In the *time* of death's coming to a person, we must
consider the sovereignty of God. He not only inflicts
death as part of the curse of the law, but He reserves to
Himself the right to limit or extend our days. The
fathers of the human race had their days lengthened
beyond what we can imagine possible in our limited
hours. God did it. Later He limited man's days to
three score years and ten. But all must needs die. It
may be said, Yes, of course, because of our condition.
True, but not primarily nor only so. We must die
because we are sinners. The termination of our natural
life is in the hand of our most holy and righteous Judge.
Here let me interject a remark, namely, the sin-bought
mortality of our bodies does not touch the natural immortality of our souls. The spirit returns to God who
gave it: the spirits of the just to Abraham's bosom, the
spirit of the wicked to hell.

Now you may ask, Can anything remove death's
gloom, horror, and terribleness? Can this abhorrent
circumstance be turned into a blessing? The infallible
Bible answers the important question most definitely:
"Blessed are the dead which die in the Lord" (Rev.
xiv. 13). "Them also which sleep in Jesus will God
bring with Him" (1 Thess. iv. 14). To sleep in Jesus,
we must be united to Him, be one with Him, as we have
union set forth in Jno. xvii.

May this blessedness of death be ours. The way to it is the new birth, justification, the revelation of Christ (Jno. iii.; Rom. iv. 25; v. 1, 2; Col. i. 27).

That such an inestimable blessing may be yours and mine is the prayer of

Your affectionate friend,

Brighton, August, 1923.   J. K. POPHAM.

The New Birth.

My dear young Friends,—Another "fundamental" is to be the subject of this my monthly letter to you. The last was the Scriptures, which are able to make us wise unto salvation (2 Tim. iii. 15). In the Word of God all that is needful for us to know is taught. From that divine repertory I bring before you the fundamental of true religion—the new birth. It is vital. Without it a person has nothing, can do nothing, can think nothing with which God can be pleased. This may sound and seem a very hard and harsh saying, it is nevertheless true. It is written, "And God saw that the wickedness of man was great in the earth, and that every imagination of the thoughts of his heart was only evil continually" (Gen. vi. 5). Knowing the utter depravity of the heart, the Lord Jesus said to Nicodemus, "Verily, verily, I say unto thee, Except a man be born again, he cannot see the kingdom of God" (Jno. iii. 3). Unless regenerated, therefore, none of you can so much as see that there is another kingdom better and above the kingdoms of this world, another and a totally different life than that you, in common with all men, are living, if you are not partakers of the new and heavenly birth which Christ told Nicodemus was necessary. Unless we are new creatures, created in righteousness and true holiness, we cannot see what we may often be reading. The new creature sees God. And the light of His holiness makes manifest our poor, lost, ruined nature, and the life imparted feels it. Hence conviction of sin, and sorrow for it. Hence again, the true view of the world which lieth in wickedness, and the end of it.

From the new birth arise the spiritual appetites, longings after pardon, sanctification, and the knowledge of the glory of God in the face of Jesus Christ. Old things pass away; old views of all things, old religion, if there was a form without the power; all things become new. New feelings about God and His character, His Word, law, threatenings, promises, eternity, heaven and hell. Solemn feelings about self, a ruined nature, a wicked heart, a worldly mind, a mind that is enmity against God; condemnation is terrible in the conscience, and the holy law bends itself against the sinner.

But O, what blessings are in store for one born again! He already possesses eternal life; and the sweet manifestations of mercy, the knowledge of the Son of God, of forgiveness of all sin, and the witness and earnest of the Spirit, these blessings await the seeking one. Also promises, Christ's presence, safety in the midst of heresies and deaths by the gracious teachings of the Spirit, and good out of afflictions. These are among the blessings of the kingdom which one who is born again sees, and by faith enters into.

What better blessing can we receive from the God of all grace? May it be given to us! So prays

Your affectionate friend,

Brighton, September, 1924.   J. K. Popham.

Resurrection.

My dear young Friends,—It may seem a mere truism to say we are living in perilous times. For all men are saying so, are fearing a cataclysm—a flood—a great revolution of some kind. "Men's hearts are failing them for fear, and for looking after those things which are coming on the earth: for the powers of heaven shall be shaken" (Luke xxi. 26). Evil as the times undoubtedly are for all, I think them especially so for the young. There are whirlpools of flagrant wickedness, drawing tens of thousands into their deadly swirl. There are deep, shining, and almost undisturbed waters of deadly religious teaching, gathering into their unsuspected depths, numberless dupes. The first steals morality; the other would promise to build it up, putting it in the place of Christ's imputed righteousness. And that which makes both these dangers such an attraction is, that *you* possess the exact counterpart in your fallen nature. Who, then, can save you from either? Only the God of all grace.

I have written to you lately about several fundamentals. This month I am bringing another before you. A bishop has said that chemistry has put an end to the belief in a resurrection of this present flesh of ours. Such a statement is a very daring denial of the Spirit's teaching of the scripture which tells us we shall rise again. "For we must all appear before the judgment-seat of Christ; that every one may receive the things done in the body, according to that he hath done, whether it be good or bad" (2 Cor. v. 10). And again, "For if we believe that Jesus died and rose again, even so them also which sleep in Jesus will God bring with Him" (1 Thess. iv. 14).

The resurrection of the dead is a fundamental. It involves the resurrection of Christ. "But if there be no resurrection of the dead, then is Christ not risen." Whoever denies the resurrection of the dead is an infidel; for he denies Christ's resurrection. And as the Lord's resurrection is stated in the inspired Word to be the church's hope of resurrection, the repudiation of that glorious rising is also the destruction of her hope, and she is of all men most miserable. Read carefully 1 Cor. xv.

When I read and reflected on the above daring blasphemy, one or two questions came into my mind, as not impertinent, to be asked of the church dignitary. i. *Do you believe there is a God, an eternal, uncaused Being, omniscient, omnipotent?* ii. *Have you seen and grasped all the possibilities of omnipotence?* iii. *Is chemistry above Him to whom all things are possible?* If chemistry is made by men to oppose and contradict the Word of God, then it becomes "science falsely so

called," which the people of God are warned to avoid,
with all other vain babblings (1 Tim. vi. 20).

Let us leave the unhappy bishop to his science, and
to God the Judge of all; and turn to the infallible
Scripture, and see what it teaches with regard to the
unspeakably important subject of the resurrection of
the dead. "The belief of a general resurrection of the
dead, which will come to pass at the end of the world,
and which will be followed with an immortality of
either happiness or misery, is a principal article of
religion." This is true. When the Lord answered the
Sadducees, the materialists of His day, He said to them,
"Do ye not therefore err, because ye know not the
Scriptures, neither the power of God?" (Mark xii. 24.)
They knew not the Scriptures which teach the blessed
doctrine of hope, neither the power of God, which
would have made it plain to them. In his noble defence
of the gospel before Agrippa, Paul asked the king,
"Why should it be thought a thing incredible with you
that God should raise the dead?" Doubtless when a
sinner believes in God, with the faith of God's operation, he believes there is nothing too hard for the divine
Majesty.

The mystery of the resurrection is beyond reason, yet
there is an analogy between it and the growth of a grain
of wheat, which is sown and dies. So Paul teaches:
"But some man will say, How are the dead raised up?
and with what body do they come? Thou fool, that
which thou sowest, . . . thou sowest not that body that
shall be, but bare grain, it may chance of wheat or of
some other grain. But God giveth it a body as it hath
pleased Him, and to every seed his own body " (1 Cor.
xv. 35—38). The faith which receives this doctrine
believes that all opposition to, and denial of it, is the
result of ignorance of the Scriptures and the power of
it.

How fearful is the state of those men who know not
God, and who have pleasure in unrighteous contradiction of His Word and power! May we be *made* to

differ, and have given to us repentance toward God, and faith toward our Lord Jesus Christ.

Beware of the concision who mutilate the Holy Scripture, cutting it with the penknife of their unholy criticism, and casting the leaves into the fire of their proud enmity against God. Many years ago, a friend of mine was asked to read the work of a popular clergyman, in which God was grievously misrepresented, but he said, "Thank you, I won't try how much poison I can take without killing myself." God give you the same spirit. So desires

Your affectionate friend,

Brighton, October, 1924. J. K. POPHAM.

Sin, Salvation, etc.

1.

To my dear young Friends,—My New Year's letter must be partly, and first of all, an acknowledgment of, and thanks for, the bundle of very kind letters sent me in response to my invitation. A personal reply I am unable to send, and my correspondents are good enough not to expect one. The letters are all cordial, and full of expressions of goodwill, which I warmly reciprocate. One is glad that one's efforts to help the readers of the "Friendly Companion" are appreciated.

The letters sent me can be classified without difficulty. I. Those which more or less distinctly show the writers' condition of mind and exercises. They have had, and have, convictions of sin, not very distinct, but a sense of being wrong—sinful. They do not express any clear apprehension of God's character, and consequent fear and dread of Him. I think this last point is perceptible in many. The Holy Ghost does not appear to reveal God very clearly in the law. Perhaps it is one of the evidences of His partial withdrawing and withholding in this "day of small things." Formerly God was great and terrible to people under the law. Notwithstanding, the day of small things is not to be despised, nor the less distinct work of the Spirit on the hearts of the

people. Indeed, to be the subject of any measure of
divine teaching and dealing is an unspeakable mercy.
Some of my correspondents seem to feel guilt a burden,
and sin a plague, and greatly fear being wrong for
eternity. They have fear which hath torment, but no
comfortable, abiding hope. They arc in bondage. They
want to be convinced that they *are* convinced of sin. If
such conviction of conviction were given it would hold
them in closer bondage, and would not relieve them of
the fear of hell. They would be arguing with themselves in a circle. In their painful uncertainty they
hear ministers, and honestly and earnestly desire to
come to the light. They hear their cases set out, their
feelings, sinkings and risings, convictions, hopes and
fears, coldness and warmth, concern and indifference,
and are moved, yet they are not really helped. The
reason appears to be twofold. i. Their own judgment
is that some, if not all, of their feelings about eternal
matters are only natural, and as the distinction between
natural and spiritual religion is not drawn, as they
judge, the comfort which the ministers design does not
reach them. ii. The witness of the Spirit is lacking,
and so no rest is possible. The letters discover this.
My young friends are up and down. Not able to bear
witness to themselves, and lacking the discovery which
the Spirit alone can make of Christ as their Redeemer,
they walk in bondage.

Two words I would say to these my correspondents.
i. Painful though it is to walk in bondage, and fear
which hath torment, it is better than false liberty, better
than building on any testimony but that of the Holy
Ghost. A spirit of prayer, true spiritual violence, by
which the kingdom of heaven is taken, a God-given view
of Christ, whose blood can cleanse from all sin, whose
righteousness can justify the ungodly that believeth in
Jesus, will issue in true liberty. Power to *wait* on God
until the much-sought blessing comes is a great thing—
the gift of God. He has said they shall not be
ashamed that wait for Him. ii. It is much harder to be
ruined and utterly lost than we generally think. Look-

ing for marks of grace, evidences of being the subjects-
of God's grace, whereon to build, may often take the
mind off the "one thing needful." *Most blessed are*
marks of grace. But they are as the garnishing of the
building, springs from the fountain. The Foundation
is the Lord Jesus Christ, and He is built upon, when,
and in so far as, He is revealed; He is the Fountain
whence all streams of life, godliness, hatred of sin, love
to God, separation from the world, light to discover
good and evil, and tokens for good, flow. The solemn
and discriminating word of Christ is, "Verily, verily, I
say unto you, Except ye eat the flesh of the Son of Man,
and drink His blood, ye have no life in you" (Jno. vi.
53). This reception of a revealed Christ by precious
faith proves all previous exercises to be of God, in-
wrought by the Spirit. The separating word caused
"many of His disciples" to go back, and they walked
no more with Him (ver. 66). Left alone with the
twelve, Jesus said to them, "Will ye also go away?"
The penetrating question evoked Peter's believing
answer, "Lord, to whom shall we go? Thou hast the
words of eternal life. And we believe and are sure that
Thou art that Christ, the Son of the living God" (ver.
68, 69). They had received Christ by revelation (Matt.
xvi. 16, 17). The one word I would say to my friends,
in concluding this part of my letter, is: *The remedy for*
your sickness, fear, weakening uncertainty, is the coming
of Christ to you by divine revelation. Till that day
arrives may you have a *waiting* faith, a confessing
spirit, and a keen appetite preserved in you.

The second class of letters is composed of apprecia-
tion of the different articles in the "Friendly Companion." Some mention the Editor's letter, and some
the other articles. To one and all I offer my thanks.
If spared, and as enabled, I will, in the year we have
now entered, do my best to entertain you profitably.

To all of you my best wishes go: and my advice is:
Read the divinely inspired Book; it is "able to make
you wise unto salvation." Avoid evil company, the
Higher Critics and their evil works. Do not seek for

changes in our ordinary services; follow the ways of
our old departed leaders. Be careful in your movements in life. Providence is God's way of working in
the world. This great truth makes every step very
important.

The God of grace bless you all in this world with His
grace, His convoy of love, and His life-giving Word and
Spirit.

Your affectionate friend,

January, 1923.   J. K. POPHAM.

2.

"THOU SHALT CALL HIS NAME JESUS: FOR HE SHALL
SAVE HIS PEOPLE FROM THEIR SINS."

My dear young Friends,—The above great and heavenly
word expresses the infinite love of God. Turn to Jno.
iii. 16; 1 Jno. iv. 9, 10. The name Jesus means a
saviour, in the case of Christ it means Jehovah is salvation. Only the Lord of glory could bear such a name.
A saviour is a relative term. Some one is lost. The
Church—His people—in common with the whole world
is lost. Lost in this sense means all are lost by their
sins, lost in their sins. Again, lost, applied to men, has
a legal aspect. Adam was made under the law. He
became lost, or dead, by breaking the law. This is
the first meaning of death. Man is dead to God
because God's law pronounces him accursed (Gal. iii.
10). Then, he is dead in trespasses and sins (Eph. ii.
1). In heart and will and understanding, man is dead.
This solemn word explains the evil courses of men—the
"course of this world." Now all this is before God,
the Judge of all, and it merits His wrath, and brings
forth the threats, punishments, wars, rumours of wars,
disasters, famines, diseases of the body, dissensions in
families, and even among the Lord's people. As from
a spring, all the disobedience to parents flows. In a
word, legally, morally, and physically, we are diseased,
cursed, and dead. And this unutterably evil state spells
hell-punishment for ever. Is there any way of escape

from so awful, so deserved a punishment? Yes, there is. And it is by the Lord Jesus Christ, whose miraculous birth is set before us in this chapter (Matt. i.).

But who can express what this great Saviour must do and suffer to save the fallen Church His eternal Father gave Him to save? Holy, harmless, and separate from sinners though He was, and entirely incapable of committing sin, His Father made Him to be sin (2 Cor. v. 21). What this meant we are told in Isaiah liii. Read that most wonderful, sorrowful, glorious chapter. What it contains is beyond our comprehension. "The God and Father of our Lord Jesus Christ" said of Him at His baptism, "This is My beloved Son, in whom I am well pleased." Yet that same Father wounded, bruised, chastised, and laid stripes on that same Son. "It pleased the Lord to bruise Him; He hath put Him to grief." In suffering all this Jesus was obedient, and the end of sufferings was in His death, and in dying He was obedient to His Father's commandment (Jno. x. 17, 18; Phil. ii. 8; Heb. xii. 2). Thus Jesus saved His people from their sins. But they are all born in sin and shapen in iniquity, and dead in trespasses and sins. But this gracious Saviour is an efficacious Saviour. He gave Himself a ransom for all, to be testified in due time. "Due time" begins in regeneration. A regenerated person is a redeemed person. A regenerated sinner feels himself to be a sinner, and prays heavy prayers with the publican. Thus, if you, my young friends, have a burden of sin on your conscience, prayer will not be a mere form. "Pains of hell," pressing need, the Spirit's operation, the prayer of necessity, if not of faith to your own sense, will take you to the God of all grace, with the cry of the keeper of the prison, the innermost dungeon in which he had thrust Paul and Silas: "Sirs, what must I do to be saved?" (Acts xvi. 30.) Then will the door of faith be opened to you, and Rom. x. 13 will be on your side. Then you will go out of your legal prison as surely as Paul and Silas were released from the prison into which they had been cast (read Isaiah xlix. 9). So Jesus saves

His people from their sins by His death for them, and saves them from their felt sins by sending salvation to them by His good Spirit. Thus may you know His all-precious Name—Jesus.

Your affectionate friend,

Brighton, February, 1930.   J. K. POPHAM.

3.

My dear young Friends,—The subject of this letter is the most evil, the most gloomy, the most terrible subject in the whole of God's universe—SIN. Very little is said about it to-day. Where it is not denied, it is ignored. One would not imagine it existed if one followed the religious press of to-day. Man is always improving, according to it. By science falsely so called, by learning, by guessing about things of which they can have no knowledge, by asserting as the "assured result" of scientific investigations, that the Bible is not fully inspired, men have gone, and are ever going, astray from the religion of their forefathers. And perhaps in nothing is the deep revolt from God more manifest than in the denial of the Fall of man, therefore of sin, as God's Word speaks of it. But even those who do not deny sin, for the most part are silent about it. They speak of love, without definition of its nature, or making clear the difference between natural and spiritual love, and the proper objects of each; of union, with little discrimination of either doctrines or persons. But the ruin of human nature by the Fall of Adam, and the just imputation of the first sin of Adam to all his family is set forth in the Word of God. The corruption of each person born in sin, I want to bring before you. Sin has relation to law. Where no law is there is no transgression; sin is the transgression of the law (Rom. iv. 15; 1 Jno. iii. 4). Law means a law-Giver. The law-Giver with whom we have to do is Jehovah, who will by no means clear the guilty. Sin is born in the heart, and takes form in imagination and thought. The earliest description of it is as an inward act. "Every imagination of the thought was only evil

continually " (Gen. vi. 5). Thus thought is an action.
" Thou shalt not covet." " Whoso hateth his brother
is a murderer " (Exod. xx. 17; 1 Jno. iii. 15). To wish,
then, for something God has seen fit not to give us, is
sin. To hate a person is murder. To love the world
is to be an enemy of God (1 Jno. ii. 16). Such conduct
is punishable, it is guilt, and divine law makes escape
impossible. God will by no means (known to the law)
clear the guilty (Exod. xxxiv. 7). " Thou art of purer
eyes than to behold evil, and canst not look on
iniquity." Surely this makes our position before God
exceedingly solemn! Born in sin, living in sin because
our imaginations and thoughts are sinful, as proceeding
from a sinful nature, a bitter fountain that cannot send
forth sweet water. Out of the heart proceed evil
thoughts, murders, and all evils. Now this sinful nature
cannot change itself. " Can the Ethiopian change his
skin, or the leopard his spots ? then may ye also do good
that are accustomed to do evil " (Jer. xiii. 23). See
then the condition of fallen man. Grievous though the
very mention of it is, it is not improved by ignorance
of it, or by opposition to the truth of it, or by a denial
of its existence. Is a boy not guilty of dishonouring his
father and mother because, after the fashion of the day,
he laughs at his disobedience, and says it is nothing, or
that many others do the same ? Is the youth who steals
not guilty because he escapes detection and punishment ?
Is it quite innocent to go to the cinemas because others
go and everybody is excited and laughs ? Is Sabbath-
breaking right because the vast majority of people do
it ? Is novel-reading proper because it is popular,
because some professors indulge in it! O sin, how hast
thou blinded us, so that we do not know where we are
going, nor what will be the end! For when thou art
finished in us in this life, then death, the awful wages
of it, will be paid us.

I say, in the next place, that a sacred conviction of
sin by the Holy Ghost, a sight of it in His light, a
belief that no man can deliver his soul from the law
and its just curse, is a very great mercy. Sighs, cries,

trying to forsake sin and please God, now become the
life of the sinner. Conscience condemns him, the Word
of God wounds and distresses him, the thought of God
and the day of judgment is all but intolerable to him.
The devil will do his utmost to stifle the conviction, and
to belittle sin, but more or less distinctly the Spirit's
wound is kept open and runs in the night, and ceases
not till mercy, through the blood of Christ, heals it. If
such a wound be given any of you, you will be thankful for
it later. Sin is a bitter thing, but better to know and feel
and taste its bitterness here than endure the punishment
of it throughout eternity. Better to be a " Mr. Fearing " all your days here, than " Talkative " whose end
was destruction. Where sin is bitter, and confessed,
then pardon comes flowing from the Lord Jesus Christ.
He is exalted to be a Prince and a Saviour, for to give
repentance to Israel, and forgiveness of sins.

God bless you, dear young friends, with a thorough
conviction of sin.

Your affectionate friend,

Brighton, August, 1930.   J. K. POPHAM.

4.

My dear young Friends,—Read Genesis iii., read it
carefully. There you will see the root and spring of all
the sin that is in the world, of all that is wrong in your
own hearts and lives, the evil thoughts, desires, and
ways, and the cause of death. In Genesis ii. 16, 17,
the Holy Ghost informs us of the law which was given
to Adam: "And the Lord God commanded the man,
saying, Of every tree of the garden thou mayest freely
eat. But of the tree of the knowledge of good and
evil, thou shalt not eat of it: for in the day that thou
eatest thereof thou shalt surely die." Now Adam was
the root of all men, and he represented all men. This
is why all men die. " Wherefore, as by one man sin
entered into the world, and death by sin; and so death
passed upon all men, for that all have sinned. For
until the law sin was in the world; but sin is not
imputed when there is no law " (Rom. v. 12, 13). The

law which was before sin, and by which sin exists and is imputed, was the law given to Adam as you read just now in Genesis ii. 16, 17. Where no law is there is no transgression; for sin is the transgression of the law. "I had not known lust except the law had said, Thou shalt not covet." "As in Adam all die." In Adam all lived as in their Head. You may see this doctrine of representation illustrated in Levi, who, Paul tells us, paid tithes before he was born (Heb. vii. 9). So we obeyed in Adam while he was obedient and served God in Eden, and when in that pure, lovely, and fruitful garden he disobeyed, we disobeyed. Here, then, is the solemn scripture of original sin. We all sinned in Adam. All died in Adam. Here is the bitter root of all the sin in the world. The atheism, lust, vanity, pride, false religion, back-biting, gossip, lying, war, murder, hatred, ignorance of God, disobedience to parents, the pictures, theatres, and places of amusement and public houses. Oh, how guilty we all are! All as an unclean thing, and our righteousnesses only filthy rags. It is as true of us all as to our nature, as it was of Israel as a rebellious nation, "the whole head is sick, and the whole heart faint. From the sole of the foot even unto the head there is no soundness in it; but wounds, and bruises, and putrifying sores: they have not been closed, neither bound up, neither mollified with ointment" (Isa. i. 5, 6).

Possibly you may readily agree to this because you have read your Bibles, and heard it preached. But agreeing to it in that way only will leave you quite ignorant of it and dead in it. None but the Holy Ghost can quicken you and open your eyes to feel and see the horrid things in your hearts. God is the Fountain of life and light. It is in His light that any sinners rightly see sin. Oh the sight of hitherto-hidden monsters! It is a most sickening sight. The deeper this divine light of life penetrates, the more evils are discovered, and the brighter shines the pure justice of God into the conscience, and then the convinced sinner justifies God in the solemn, weighty, and awful sentence of eternal death. Sin, death, and hell are realities, seen, felt, and feared. And until the Divine, divinely-given Substitute is manifested by His Spirit there is neither hope, nor comfortable access to God, nor peace, nor rest. The Son of God is His Father's salvation unto the ends of the earth. He invites burdened, labouring souls to come to Himself, and the invitation is given with power. Where the word of a King is there is power. The invited sinner says, "Lo, glad I come." It is wonderful to feel the load of sin and guilt taken from the conscience, and the peace of God, which passeth all understanding, keeping the heart and mind by Jesus Christ. It is good to say feelingly:

> "Of this the best of men have need,
> This I the worst receive."

May God the Holy Ghost convince you of sin if it please Him, and then take of the things of Christ and show them to you. In such a merciful case you will while here feel the truth of Paul's word: "I am carnal, sold under sin; the good that I would I do not. O wretched man that I am, who shall deliver me from the body of this death?" And by sweet occasions sing, "I thank God through Jesus Christ; so then with the mind I myself serve the law of God, but with the flesh the law of sin." God bless you all.

Your affectionate friend,

Brighton, May, 1931.　　　　　　　　J. K. POPHAM.

5.

My dear young Friends,—The theme of this letter is an attractive one to some people. The name of it is "SALVATION." It has an invincible attraction to people who are led to see that it is a relative term, that it relates to the condition they are taught to know they are in. They are ruined, lost, hopeless and helpless in themselves. Then they are led by the Spirit of Christ to see the Saviour of sinners. Of the Virgin Mary the angel of the Lord said: "And she shall bring forth a

Son, and thou shalt call His Name JESUS; for He shall save His people from their sins " (Matt. i. 21). Thus you will see that salvation is a relative term. It is connected with the terrible state of mankind as lying in wickedness, as transgressors of God's holy law. In no way but that which God planned, could salvation be brought to His people: viz., by the gift of His Son, the sending of Him into this world that they might live through Him (1 Jno. iv. 9). Salvation is the saving *from* sin. Salvation from sin in the guilt of it. This could only be by the death of the Lord Jesus Christ, the only-begotten Son of God. "But when the fulness of the time was come, God sent forth His Son, made of a woman, made under the law, to redeem them that were under the law, that we might receive the adoption of sons " (Gal. iv. 4, 5). This was the only way by which the guilt of sin could be removed from God's people.

The second thing in salvation, is salvation from the power and pollution of sin. "By nature we are all dead in trespasses and sins, wherein we walk according to the course of this world, according to the prince of the power of the air." This is a terrible state; the power, the dominion of sin no man can break. It follows of a gracious and just necessity that the people whose guilt the Lord of glory removed by death should be born again, have a new heart given to them, new eyes and new ears. Now is sin seen, felt, and mourned over. "What fruit had ye then in those things whereof ye are now ashamed ? " (Rom. vi. 21.) Seeing themselves in the broad way that leadeth to destruction, and being alarmed, they strive to enter in at the strait gate and narrow way, which leadeth unto life, and which is found by few. If we are born again we feel our con-demnation, feel the law demands from us what we cannot give it. "There is none good but One, that is God; but if thou wilt enter into life, keep the com-mandments " (Matt. xix. 17—19). This deep-reaching, penetrating word cuts off all hope of self-help. Salva-tion must come from without, even from the Saviour of His people. The power of sin is felt just as the law is felt, the dominion of sin is felt just as the law comes and lays its claim on our consciences. If we can honestly say we would not, we have to say we cannot. If we would flee from a besetting sin, we find it is too powerful for us to overcome. If we would believe in God we find an infidel heart asking with devilish enmity, " Who is the Lord ? " saying with an unknown truth, " We know not the Lord." If we would be humble, pride rises and asserts itself, as if independence belonged to a creature, or that it is in a man that walketh to direct his steps. From this inbred power of sin the Lord alone can save us. And His promise to His people is that sin shall not have dominion over them, because they are not under the law, but under grace.

Then there is the pollution of sin. This, when felt, shuts the soul up in a painful sense of unfitness to pray. For holiness becometh God's house or presence. For this woeful state the precious blood of Christ is sufficient. " If we confess our sins, He is faithful and just to forgive us our sins, and to cleanse us from all unrighteousness." And that no regenerated person shall miss the strait gate and narrow way and die under the power of sin, and no sensible filthy soul sink into hell in his confessed pollution, the Holy Ghost is given to glorify Christ as a Saviour (Jno. xvi. 7—15). It is thus the people of God are saved by the Lord and Saviour Jesus Christ.

What a mercy it will be if we are brought to know our ruin by sin, our hopeless and helpless state of guilt, and the dominion and pollution of sin. There will go up to God the publican's cry from our hearts, " God be merciful to me a sinner," and then will come into our hearts the most blessed experience of that favoured man, who went down to his house justified.

God give this salvation to my young friends. Amen.

Your affectionate friend,

Brighton, July, 1931.   J. K. POPHAM.

6.

My dear young Friends,—Eternity is a mystery; a terror to the sinner dead in trespasses and sins, as it may obtrude itself upon his mind, though the devil will, if possible, keep it out. But eternity is inevitable. We must enter into a state which will never end. We must live either in heaven or in hell for ever and ever; either be like Christ by the imputation of His righteousness, and the cleansing efficacy of His blood, and the quickening power of the Holy Ghost, whereby the soul is created in righteousness and true holiness (Eph. iv. 24), or appear in our own filthy garments and be lost for ever.

Now the fact being that we must needs die and be as water spilt upon the ground that cannot be gathered up again, in this time state the weighty question is, have we any reason within our hearts to hope that death will be a gain to us? There is a scripture which tells us that Christ came to seek and to save that which was lost (Luke xix. 10). It is clear that the "lost" in this verse are not the souls now in perdition. But the lost in sin, the elect of God who are children of wrath (Eph. ii. 3). Lost, as to the knowledge of either themselves or God; lost, as to right desires, faith, hope, love, and all righteousness. Even if there is a measure of natural knowledge of God, they glorify Him not as God, but are vain in their imaginations, and their foolish hearts are darkened (Rom. i. 21). Such were, and are, the "lost" whom Christ came to seek and save. They were always in His heart, purpose, and grace. To save them, He, who is the Son of God in His divine Person, became Man that He might bear their sins in His own body on the tree (1 Peter ii. 24). Thus He sought His lost sheep and saved them. Now this involves another seeking and saving. Every one of them is dead in trespasses and sins, and says in his heart to God, "Depart from me, for I desire not the knowledge of Thy ways." If he has godly parents the fact makes no difference; though he may be under proper restraint, he chafes under it. Having the world in his heart, the

external draws him, and the god of this world, the
prince of the power of the air, drives him. The devil
is a hard master, yet his subjects know it not, do not
believe it. But these " lost " ones are always in God's eye.
The bounds of their running from the Divine Majesty
are fixed, they cannot go beyond them. The Saviour
seeks them on the dark mountains of their folly and
madness. He found about three thousand of them in
Jerusalem on the day of Pentecost (Acts ii. 41). He
found Saul of Tarsus when he was pursuing his mad,
murderous course (Acts ix. 3—5). He made use of
Paul to find Timothy. He finds and saves the " lost "
to-day. They are regenerated. Then begin their
troubles, the pains of hell, the sorrows of death. What
sights they get, by the Spirit, of a holy God, angry in
His law, demanding payment of all they owe Him, and
convinced they cannot pay Him. In some cases great
terror is felt, anger, because, as they judge and feel,
they are made for the day of evil, because, too, the
Lord taketh not pleasure in the legs of a man, and
teaches them it is not of him that runneth nor willeth,
but of God that sheweth mercy (Rom. ix. 16). How
angry this passage has made some! But all this work
is to kill a man to himself, to the law: " I through the
law "—its action in my conscience—" am dead to the
law." All this is the seeking the lost in a painful way
of experience. The saving comes by the gospel being
made the power of God unto salvation. The Spirit of
Christ gives glimpses of Him in His all-sufficiency.
Oh, this draws the lost soul, inspires prayer for a full
pardon, and when this prayer is answered, the saved
one goes forth in the dances of them that make merry.
Then the Lord Jesus Christ is all in all. There is no
mixing of law and gospel, of faith and works. No
flesh is to glory in God's sight (1 Cor. i. 30, 31). He
knows how the matter stands with us, whether we have
been found by the heavenly Seeker who cannot err, or
whether we are dead in trespasses and sins. If the
latter, how awful is our present case. The Lord is
able to change it. None else can. Some of you may

have been brought up in the nurture and admonition of the Lord, but, good as that is, it is not being found, born again, it is not being washed, sanctified, justified in the Name of the Lord Jesus, and by the Spirit of our God (1 Cor. vi. 11). For fallen nature is the same in all the children of Adam (Rom. v. 12). Oh, it is dreadful to be sinners, but more dreadful still not to know that we are sinners, deserving endless punishment. Oh but it is, and will be, a wonder of everlasting love, grace, and wisdom, if we are sought and saved.

God bless you, my young readers.

Your affectionate friend,

Brighton, September, 1931. J. K. Popham.

Three Faiths.

1.

My dear young Friends,—According to Holy Scripture the subject of faith is of the first importance. God has made much to hang on it. Men have wrought wonders by it. It is one of the two essentials of true religion: repentance toward God, and faith toward our Lord Jesus Christ. It is the gift of God. Christ is the Author and Finisher of it. It is the effect of the same glorious power which God wrought in Christ when He raised Him from the dead. No wonder should it be that it is called the faith of the operation of God, and, again, the faith of God's elect. And because every sinner who possesses this faith is delivered from the power and kingdom of Satan, and turns from idols to serve the living and true God, and to wait for His Son from heaven, whom He raised from the dead, even Jesus, which delivered us from the wrath to come, that arch-enemy of God and man makes war against every God-made believer. Hence there are various counterfeits of faith in the world, and sought to be passed in the camp of the saints. Only two kinds of faith I shall generally notice in this letter, as all others will be more or less distinctly found in the two.

1. *Historical faith.* This is in a sense a true faith.

It takes its stand on the Word of God; it holds as true
the account of the creation by the Word of God; it
admires providence in thousands of indubitable instances
as narrated in that blessed Book; it believes in the
birth, life, and death of Jesus, and His resurrection,
together with the proofs that He who appeared to Mary
Magdalene, who entered the room where His disciples
were assembled, who led them out as far as to Bethany,
and blessed them, and then was parted from them, and
carried up into heaven, was the same identical Person
on whose sacred, agonised body they had gazed on
Calvary's cross. Historical faith as thus viewed is
good. It is rational, beautiful, becoming men, inasmuch
as it honours God in His works and Word. The man
who thus believes, though he may make no open profession of God's Name, knows Him more than the so-
called religious teacher who sets out to discredit the
inspired Word of God, dishonours Christ's Person and
reduces His vicarious death to an example. I hope *all*
my young friends possess this historical faith. It dwells
in your general understanding, it influences your attitude to the Bible and public worship. *But it is lacking
an essential in you, if it goes no further.* It does not
touch your conscience, does not convince you of your
sinfulness, nor show you your sins and transgression.
In a word, it does not bring you to perceive your rela-
lationship as guilty persons to God. Thus it falls
unspeakably, sadly short. While therefore you differ
fundamentally from the Modernist, the Deist, the Socinian, the Arminian, you are not true Christians, not
believers in the scriptural sense of that wonderful name.
May the Lord give you to see the vital difference there is
between a merely rationally informed understanding and
a regenerated conscience; between an acquired knowledge of the Bible, if it be alone, and a new-born person
in the blessed sense of Jno. i. 12, 13; between admiring
the Messiah, and receiving the Son of God as made
flesh, dwelling in His Church, there declaring His
Father, and preparing her for the place He has gone to
prepare for her.

I must defer what I have to say about yet a second
sort of faith for my next letter, if it please God to spare
and enable me to write another to you. Meanwhile, I
am,

Your affectionate friend,

Brighton, October, 1927.   J. K. POPHAM.

2.

My dear young Friends,—Another kind of faith is
called *Temporary Faith*, so called because it "dureth
for a while." Then some trial or trouble arises connected with the profession made, and "by and by" the
hearer is offended, and his religion withers away. This
kind of faith appears to be the result of hearing the
Word (Matt. xiii.). Of four hearers, three were wrong.
It is probable that the wayside hearer is just a worldly
person who of custom hears preaching, but his hearing
is like seed falling on the road or the path between
open fields. No impression is made, and the seed lying
exposed is soon picked up by the birds. Many, no
doubt, hear preaching in that way: their minds, like a
popular road, full of traffic, are busy with their worldly
concerns, their business, or their pleasure. And the
devil, the wicked one, fills their ears with very pleasant
sounds of worldly things, so that there is no room for
one divine word, or thought of eternity. Such hearers
corrupt themselves, whose fruit withereth, without fruit,
twice dead, plucked up by the roots. But when the
Lord comes to execute judgment upon all, and to convince all that are ungodly among the saints, of all their
ungodly deeds which they have committed, and of all
their hard speeches which ungodly sinners have spoken
against Him, it will be more tolerable for Tyre and
Sidon at the judgment than for them. But the second
hearer differs very considerably from the first. He
receives the preached Word, he feels it, tastes of its
sweetness, and rejoices in it. Confidence is soon felt,
and a profession is easily made. He associates with the
saints, and is reckoned one of them. This, while it
occasions joy, exposes him to trouble. His family, his

friends are offended, his worldly interests are imperilled; his joy declines, and as he is not "a plant of the Lord's right hand planting," he receives no showers of blessing, no communications from Him, no "supply of the Spirit of Christ," and he withers away. He was never wounded, was never healed. He boasted of a Saviour, yet he was never "lost" in the gospel sense of that word. The third hearer is like the second in *receiving* the Word, but differs in some respects. Some promise of the fear of God appears on the surface, a quick growth in knowledge of the truth, for he is rich, no doubt educated, he can talk of things heavenly, and of the earth, with equal facility. He appears not to suffer persecution because of the Word, and the church might have entertained a good opinion of him. But after a time a coolness is found in him, his conversation is not in heaven. He has great interests in the world, to them he must give more time, thought, and close attention; he is careful about many things. He prospers, and as riches increase he sets his heart upon them, and they deceive him, he runs after the pleasures of this life, and soon gold glitters and shines in his eyes more than Christ crucified, and the gospel he professed and talked well about is choked, and he becomes changed, becomes unfruitful. In this parable there is the most striking, solemn, and awful illustration of *Temporary Faith.* May the Lord make them examples unto us, cause them to admonish us, and work in us a godly fear of coming short of His glory.

One or two other Scripture cases in which a nonenduring faith is set forth, we must look at. The first is in John's Gospel. By a miracle the Lord Jesus fed thousands of hungry people. This caused them to follow Him, and they obtained the honourable name of disciples. But when He taught them that unless they received and ate His flesh and drank His blood they were dead, they were offended, and went back, and walked no more with Him (Jno. vi. 66). Demas, coupled with Luke, the beloved physician (Col. iv. 14), is, a few years later, a castaway: "Demas hath forsaken me, having loved this present world" (2 Tim. iv. 10). What countless victims the world claims from the professing church! The same lips may cry, "Hosanna to the Son of David!" and, "Away with Him, crucify Him!" The pharisee's faith took him up into the temple to pray, but it did not carry him to the throne of grace. Balaam talked of God, and professed a desire to obey Him, but he loved the wages of unrighteousness. Simon, the sorcerer, believed and was baptised, and continued with Philip and wondered, beholding the miracles and signs which were done; but his heart was not right in the sight of God (Acts viii. 13—22). Ananias and Sapphira were believers for a season, but their love of money pierced them through with eternal sorrow (Acts v.). *Temporary Faith* cannot bring the sinner before God, viewing, feeling, and confessing original sin and personal transgessions, nor can it wait for justification, the need of which is not felt.

Well, indeed, will it be for us, dear young friends, if the faith of God's elect, and of the operation of the Holy Ghost, be wrought in us. For then we shall tremble before His holy Majesty, and at His word of threatening, and strive to enter in at the strait gate, and be found in the narrow way that leadeth unto life everlasting. Thus, and thus alone, can men believe to the saving of the soul (Heb. x. 39). Amen.

Your affectionate friend,
Brighton, November, 1927.   J. K. POPHAM.

3.

My dear young friends,—After the two kinds of faith I have spoken of in two previous letters, there remains another kind to bring before you. This I will call *True Faith*, because it does not wither away in time of trial. It keeps the followers of the Lamb at His side, under His glorious banner (Rev. xvii. 14). The Scripture calls it "The faith of God's elect" (Titus i. 1), because they alone have it given to them: "For by grace are ye saved through faith, and that not of yourselves: it is the gift of God" (Eph. ii. 8). Thus they

are distinguished from the "dead in trespasses and
sins," among whom they once were (Eph. ii. 3). This
wonderful grace is also called "The faith of the operation of God" (Col. ii. 12). It is called into being by
the Holy Ghost, and it stands in His power (1 Cor. ii.
5). It thus differs in its birth and working from all
merely human ideas, understanding, beliefs, and per-
suasions; it comes from heaven, and its conversation is
in heaven (Phil. iii. 20; 2 Cor. iv. 18; see also Heb.
xi.). By it the word of Christ is proved to be true:
"That which is born of the flesh is flesh; and that
which is born of the Spirit is spirit;" the flesh will ever
remain flesh, nothing better, nothing else. And the
solemn distinction must remain. Hence the sword, the
fire, which the Lord sends, the enmity between the two
seeds. There is yet another name given by the Holy
Ghost to the faith of God's elect. By the apostle Peter
He calls it "Precious Faith." The apostles, and the
"about three thousand souls," and many others, had
received the divine gift, and now to the "strangers
scattered throughout Pontus, Galatia, Cappadocia, Asia,
and Bithynia," the Lord had given the same inestimable
gift (2 Peter i. 1). On account of its divine Author and
Finisher this faith is precious. All His works are
great and glorious, and in an especial manner faith is
so, inasmuch as it has Himself, as the God of salvation,
for its proper Object and End. His glorious Person,
His finished work on earth, His universal dominion in
heaven and earth, His gospel, grace, promises, and
precepts, these all are faith's food, strength, comfort,
and delight. By it the work of Christ, as well as His
Person, becomes a reality in the soul: "Now faith is the
substance of things hoped for, the evidence of things not
seen" (Heb. xi. 1). The whole of that wonderful
chapter is a striking illustration of the first verse. The
things, the truths, the commandments, the promises, the
victory over dead bodies, the seeing the Invisible, and
the consequent endurance, the subduing of kingdoms,
the courage to face fire, endure death rather than obtain
a dishonourable and only temporary deliverance, are all

ascribed to the wonderful grace of faith, because they were a reality in the soul, the understanding, and the conscience of believers.

Seeing that true faith is such a powerful instrument for good in the soul, that it deals with God, and holds the truths which it pleases Him in His love to give to His people, we may well ask if He has been gracious to *us* in the bestowment of such a blessing. By it the Lord Jesus is known as suitable for *sinners*. And if we have faith we *know* and *feel* that we are sinners. Indeed, if we do not know and feel that we are lost, Christ will be only a name to us; we shall never come to Him, never abide in Him, never love Him. His faith is a gift beyond price. He is exalted to give it, as well as repentance (Acts v. 31).

Now this blessed faith will, if you possess it, preserve you from the terrible errors of these perilous times. It will enable you to receive and hold the account of creation as given by divine inspiration in Genesis i., and reject and hate Evolutionism. It will cause you to believe in the Incarnation of the Son of God, and His substitution for His own people, His vicarious death for them, and His ascension into heaven, there to intercede for them, and at last to receive them to Himself. It will enable you to believe in the Holy Ghost, and seek His most merciful indwelling. And the fruits of grace, the work of faith, will be found in you. What better wish then can I have for you, and express in prayer to God for you, than that you may be blest with the inestimable, the free grace gift of the faith of God's elect?

Your affectionate friend,

Brighton, December, 1927.   J. K. POPHAM.

Two Peoples.

My dear young Friends,—I want to bring before you a strong contrast between two peoples. i. Look at the people of God. They are called the people whom He hath chosen for His own inheritance, whom He hath blest with all spiritual blessings in heavenly places or

things in Christ. In Christ they have eternal life:
" And this is the record, that God hath given to us
eternal life, and this life is in His Son " (1 Jno. v. 11).
And this " eternal life " is communicated to each of
them by the Holy Ghost, as it is written, " Which were
born, not of blood, nor of the will of the flesh, nor of
the will of man, but of God " (Jno. i. 13). By the
Lord Jesus Christ His people are forgiven all their
sins: " Him hath God exalted with His right hand to
be a Prince and a Saviour, for to give repentance to
Israel, and forgiveness of sins " (Acts v. 31). For them
Christ, as their Intercessor, prays: " I pray for them "
(John xvii. 9). " Who shall lay anything to the charge
of God's elect ? It is God that justifieth. Who is he
that condemneth ? It is Christ that died, yea rather,
that is risen again, who is even at the right hand of
God, who also maketh intercession for us " (Rom. viii.
33, 34). They are kept from evil and the destroyer by
the power of God: " Who are kept by the power of God
through faith unto salvation, ready to be revealed in the
last time " (1 Pet. i. 5). Waters and rivers cannot
drown them, fire cannot consume them, for their Lord
their God is with them (Isa. xliii. 2, 3). They are
guided by the Lord: " I will instruct thee, and teach
thee in the way which thou shalt go: I will guide thee
with Mine eye " (Psa. xxxii. 8). These favoured people
have mansions prepared for them, and none shall miss
their way, for the eye of the Lord is upon them, and
His ear is open unto their cry (Psa. xxxiii. 18); and
when the appointed time arrives He will come and
receive them to Himself (Jno. xiv. 3). It is no wonder
that Moses, seeing in the light of God the blessedness of
the family of God, and the recompense of the reward,
exclaimed: " Happy art thou, O Israel: who is like unto
thee, O people saved by the Lord, the Shield of thy
help, and who is the Sword of thine excellency! and
thine enemies shall be found liars unto thee: and thou
shalt tread upon their high places " (Deut. xxxiii. 29).

ii. Now look at another people, the world. They are
in wickedness, " the whole world lieth in wickedness "

(1 Jno. v. 19). This is the entire course of the world, who are under the prince of the power of the air (Eph. ii. 2; vi. 12). They are carnally minded, which is death (Rom. viii. 6); blinded by sin and Satan, the god of this world; gross darkness covers them. They are under the curse, for it is written, "Cursed is every one that continueth not in all things which are written in the book of the law to do them" (Gal. iii. 10; Deut. xxvii. 26). Christ does not pray for *them*, "I pray not for the world" (Jno. xvii. 9). At the judgment they are to be cast out into outer darkness, and remain there (Rev. xxii. 11).

What a contrast! Righteous or unrighteous; loved or hated; chosen and called, or left in sin, guilt and condemnation; sheep or goats; the people of the blessing, or the people against whom the Lord hath indignation for ever!

How many of us can say, do say, each for himself:

"Pause, my soul, and ask the question,
Art thou ready to meet God?
Am I made a real Christian,
Wash'd in the Redeemer's blood?
Have I union
To the Church's living Head?"

How many of us can pray, do pray:

"Prepare me, gracious God,
To stand before Thy face:
Thy Spirit must the work perform,
For it is all of grace"?

It is an unspeakable mercy to have our eyes opened to see the blessed state the Lord's people are in, and to be led to pray, "Remember me, O Lord, with the favour that Thou bearest unto Thy people: O visit me with Thy salvation; that I may see the good of Thy chosen, that I may rejoice in the gladness of Thy nation, that I may glory with Thine inheritance" (Ps. cvi. 4, 5).

It will be a wonder of everlasting love to be found in Christ, and hear Him say, "I am thy salvation."

I am, Your affectionate friend and well-wisher,
Brighton, April, 1921. J. K. POPHAM.

Providence.

My dear young Friends,—Whether we believe it or not, we are under the all-controlling providence of God, "For in Him we live, and move, and have our being" (Acts xvii. 28). "Holy Scripture alone accounts for providence in its infinite variety, its seeming inequality. (Read Job xi. 6—12; Matt. xx. 15.)"—So I wrote in my letter of March last. And it is to this amazing, penetrating, all-reaching, and humbling subject my letter this month shall be devoted. It is an awe-inspiring thought, when thought of it is correct. The Psalmist felt it so. Read carefully Ps. cxxxix. What he was, what he thought, where he went, or thought of going, to avoid the divine presence, he found the Lord was there. Only faith could praise God for this wondrous omniscience.

Wondering how to define providence to you, the beautiful, full, and noble Westminster Confession of Faith came to my memory, and I here give it to you: "God, the great Creator of all things, doth uphold, direct, dispose, and govern all creatures, actions, and things, from the greatest even to the least, by His most wise and holy providence, according to His infallible foreknowledge, and the free and immutable counsel of His own will, to the praise of the glory of His wisdom, power, justice, goodness, mercy."

Now this holy, wise, and mysterious work of providence is carried on by the Lord Jesus Christ. Having purged the sins of His church, and thus purchased her with His own blood (Acts xx. 28), He received "all power in heaven and earth," "a Name which is above every name; that at the Name of Jesus every knee should bow, of things in heaven, and things in earth, and things under the earth: and that every tongue should confess that Jesus Christ is Lord, to the glory of God the Father" (Matt. xxviii. 18; Phil. ii. 9—11). How worthy is the Lord of life to receive and exercise this universal dominion, and adoration and plaudits of the heavenly hosts; we hear, as it were, the loud song, "Worthy is the Lamb that was slain to receive power, and riches, and wisdom, and honour, and glory, and blessing " (Rev. v. 12). The obedience there is perfect, willingness being part of it. On earth some render the same service, but it is obedience to the faith, and is imperfect. From all others an unknowing, an unwilling service is compelled. The will of God is not done from the heart.

Christ's authority is over those men's thoughts and actions who fear Him not in their ways. Balaam wishes to curse Israel; his tongue is used to express some of the greatest blessings the church of God enjoys, (Num. xxii.—xxiv.). Elimelech leaves his famine-stricken country with his wife and two sons, in order that Ruth, the "Moabitish damsel," shall be brought to Bethlehem, and become an ancestress of Christ. The king of Assyria is sent to punish Israel, but he knows not that that is his mission: "Howbeit he meaneth not so, neither doth his heart think so; but it is in his heart to destroy and cut off nations not a few. . . . Wherefore it shall come to pass, that when the Lord hath performed His whole work upon Mount Zion and on Jerusalem, I will punish the fruit of the stout heart of the king of Assyria, and the glory of his high looks " (Isa. x.). The envy of his brethren sells Joseph to the Ishmaelites, and they, in turn, sell him to Potiphar in Egypt. Later, a famine was over all the face of the earth, involving Jacob and his family, and compelling him to send his sons down to Egypt to buy corn. But only the Lord knew that all this matter, so painful, was to bring Abraham's seed to be a stranger in a land that was not theirs, to serve them, and afflict them four hundred years, as foretold (Gen. xxxvii., xv. 13). Saul of Tarsus goes, armed with authority, to Damascus, to persecute the saints there. He knows not who will meet with him, and speak to him, change his heart, convert him, and make him an apostle. The "all power " of Christ was manifested.

The providence of our great God and Saviour Jesus Christ is seen in the way He has directed the thoughts and steps of one to Himself, as yet unknown (Luke xix.

1—6; Jno. i. 47—49). Or of one of His servants to meet with a vessel of mercy, in order to fill him with mercy (Acts viii. 25—39).

Sometimes the Sovereign Ruler has permitted trouble and bereavements to befal some of His to show His power over disease and death (Matt. xiv. 30, 31; Mark i. 30, 31; Matt. viii. 5—10; xv. 22, 28; Mark v. 15).

He rules over devils; they cannot enter a herd of swine without His permission (Mark v. 12). They cannot remain in a person longer than Christ allows them (Matt. xvii. 18; Luke iv. 36).

He compassionately feeds hungry people (Matt. xv. 32—38). He raises the dead (Jno. xi. 43).

When the Lord will send His gospel to the Gentiles, the disciples shall be scattered from Jerusalem by persecution (Acts viii. 1—4). How quietly they might have remained there for a while, but the Lord must be preached to the Gentiles, for He is Lord of all. " He shall speak peace unto the heathen: and His dominion shall be from sea to sea, and from the river unto the ends of the earth " (Zech. ix. 10). Thus began to be fulfilled God's covenant with Abram: " And in thee shall all the families of the earth be blessed " (Gen. xii. 3).

This is the great God, our all-sufficient One, to whom Jeremiah adoringly speaks thus: " Who would not fear Thee, O King of nations ? for to Thee doth it appertain: forasmuch as among all the wise men of the nations, and in all their kingdoms, there is none like unto Thee " (Jer. x. 7). All men are brutish compared with Him. " I, even I, am the Lord; and beside Me there is no Saviour " (Isa. xliii. 11—17).

I will close this letter by giving you some passages of Scripture to look up and read, in which, if you have the seeing eye and the hearing ear (Prov. xx. 12), you may see and hear Him, to whom all power and dominion are given: Dan. vii. 13, 14; Matt. xi. 27; xxviii. 18; Luke i. 32; x. 22; Jno. iii. 35; xiii. 3; xvii. 2; Acts ii. 36; Rom. xiv. 9; 1 Cor. xv. 25—28; Eph. i. 10—20, 21, 22; Phil. ii. 9—11; Heb. i. 2; ii. 8; 1 Pet. iii. 22; Rev. v.; xvii. 14. I have thus proved the proposition with which I started this letter: "Holy Scripture alone accounts for providence in all its infinite variety, its seeming inequality." Of course, the points are not elaborated, the small space at my disposal forbids that. But if you are enabled to consider the passages of Scripture to which you are referred, you will have a fair knowledge of the very large and important doctrine of divine providence.

Oh that we may be blessed with the grace of this glorious Christ! Then will all His providences toward and with us be found working for our good; and gladly from time to time, by His Spirit's power, we shall bow before and worship, and follow Him, and trust Him.

Your affectionate friend,

Brighton, June, 1924. J. K. POPHAM.

On Holidays, etc.

My dear young Friends,—I am reminded in many ways that the holiday season has commenced, and one of those reminders is caused by two facts. One is the absence on Sunday of some of my young friends from our usual services, and that gives rise to the question, "Where is So-and-so?" and the answer at once is, "Away on holiday." I am thankful to be able to say of many that invariably if they are not in their usual places, the cause is either through illness or absence from home. The second fact is that I see some strangers in the pews, and that means some friends have come to spend their holiday at Brighton, and have sought out the chapel which they wish to attend. I remember a friend once telling me, upon her first visit to the town, that she had been to the chapel beforehand, in order to find out its exact whereabouts, and the time of the services, so as to be in order on Sunday.

Now I think you will have already guessed why I am writing this to you. You, my dear young friends, living in different parts of the country, have, perhaps, already started your summer holiday, and others will be taking theirs in turn. What I want to impress upon you is this. Before you decide where to go, *think about*

the Sundays, and make sure that the beautiful scenery
you hope to enjoy, the change of air and of companionship to which you are looking forward, shall also in-
clude provision for the Lord's Day. Go where you know
there is a chapel where the truth is preached, and once
having ascertained this before making your decision as
to where to go, be in that place of worship, as at home
on Sunday. Let your Sundays be well spent, and the
remaining six days of the week will be all the more
beneficial to you in every way. I pray that your
whole holiday may indeed be spent, as I desire all our
days may be, in the fear of the Lord, and then I know
that your tastes will be influenced aright. You will
avoid those pleasures which bring no good with them,
those companions who will lead you astray, and those
books which are harmful. You will seek instead the
highest, the purest and the best, and you will return
from your holiday, by God's blessing, stronger and
better in every way.

You have my best wishes at all times, and you have
them now. May God bless you all while on your holi-
days, and bring you all home once more in safety, and
to your accustomed seats in chapel!

Your affectionate friend,

Brighton, July, 1924.   J. K. POPHAM.

Our Duty and Accountability.

" Let us hear the conclusion of the whole matter: Fear
God, and keep His commandments; for this is the
whole duty of man. For God shall bring every work
into judgment, with every secret thing, whether it be
good, or whether it be evil."—ECCLES. xii. 13, 14.

My dear young Friends,—This inspired scripture is
very comprehensive. No single thing in the life of any
one of us is beyond its reach. Internal and external
actions come within its scope and vision. It is ex-
pounded by another word of infallible Scripture: " Thou
shalt love the Lord thy God with all thy heart, and with
all thy soul, and with all thy strength, and with all thy
mind; and thy neighbour as thyself " (Luke x. 27). By

this passage we may see that the whole duty of each of us falls into three parts. i. Love to God. He claims our love, and that not loosely. We are to love Him within the boundary He Himself has fixed—our entire being, heart, soul, strength, and mind. Our being, His good gift, He claims. Adam, pure, upright, newly from the Creator's hand, was made for Him, and was called on to give himself to Him in the prescribed service. To us, his children, the same law comes and demands the same service, that is love. For we show the work of the law written in our hearts, the evidence of it being the witness of our conscience in either accusations or excuses (Rom. ii. 14, 15). Nor can we plead ignorance of God. For the knowledge of Him is within the reach of each of us: "Because that which may be known of God is manifest in them: for God hath showed it unto them. For the invisible things of Him from the creation of the world are clearly seen, being understood by the things that are made, even His eternal power and Godhead; so that they are without excuse" (Rom. i. 19, 20). By creation God manifested His power, wisdom, and goodness, in making suitable and ample provision for all His creatures, and by His providence, ruling and guiding all things to an ordained end, showing His will, sovereignty and beneficence; thus He emphasises His claim to our love. The boundary of love is, as before said, our whole being, our duty is as deep, high, broad, and long as our heart, soul, strength, and mind. He is to be supreme. Every creature, pleasure, duty, work, aim, thought, and word, must be subordinated to this one duty; it is the whole duty of man. It includes the fear of God, worship, and submission to His revealed will. As in His nature He is the Alpha and the Omega, so He must be to us in the whole of our lives.

ii. The second branch of our duty is to love our neighbour as ourselves. "Therefore all things whatsoever ye would that men should do to you, do ye even so to them; for this is the law and the prophets" (Matt. vii. 12). This is a comprehensive word. Whatever self-love, dear interest, beneficent action, tender consideration, noble allowance, attributing of proper motives as far as possible which we would claim for ourselves, it is our duty to give to others. A neighbour may be poor, afflicted, hungry, and in such a state as to excite pity. In such a case we are not to wholly reap the corners of our fields, nor gather every grape of our vineyard, but leave them for the poor and stranger, yea, if our *enemy* hunger and thirst, we are to feed him and give him drink.

iii. This commanded neighbourly love is to be equal to the love of self. What a word! To what natural man does it not seem more proper and just to consider self first? But the law of God does not allow that. What do I need? My neighbour needs the same. Am I sick? He may be also. Am I in trouble or sorrow? His case may be equal to mine or worse. Is my way in providence perplexed and dark? His may be also. What then? Just what I need and desire for myself I am to extend to him in my heart, if there be not power in my hand to do it. Do I demand that men should deal justly by me? I must equally demand of myself that I mete the same measure of justice to him.

This is the law, this is the whole duty of man. Who meets it and answers to it? Man is fallen. But the fall and utter ruin we are all involved in, does not change the law one jot or tittle, does not therefore reduce in the least our duty, nor absolve us from our relation to our Maker—the relation of subjects. For a moment let us reflect on our position as under the law. (*a*) We are guilty of innumerable transgressions, we are always adding sin to sin; for there is no man that doeth good and sinneth not. (*b*) We are hopeless and helpless. The law can give us no relief. Its only function, in case of a breach in it, is to condemn. The law is holy, just, and good, but having killed us in its sentence, it cannot give life. (*c*) Therefore we, as guilty persons, are in the hands of God, who says He will by no means clear the guilty. It is impossible to imagine a worse case out of hell than ours. We are under a law that can do nothing, but curse us for every transgression (Gal. iii. 10). But, glory be to God! He Himself has found a ransom, has laid help on one that is mighty. If then we are born again, convinced of sin, and feel as did the terrified jailor, lost and ready to perish, and cry out with him, "What must I do to be saved?" the Holy Ghost who has given the conviction and the cry will reveal the divine answer—the blood of Jesus Christ, His Son, cleanseth from all sin. May rich mercy, relief, and salvation be given to each.

Thus prays　　　　Your affectionate friend,
Brighton, March, 1930.　　　　J. K. POPHAM.

Beginnings.

My dear young Friends,—The beginning of the new year occasioned many thoughts of many things, both of my own and those of others. And among them were thoughts about the beginning of things. Our lives, our school days, the development of our minds, the wishes, plans, and hopes of youth; the beginning of a business or a profession with us. With some of us the beginning of convictions of sin, of confession of sin, of forsaking the world, both of necessity and of choice. The beginning of hope in the mercy of God, the first openings of some scriptures, and of first views of Christ. Such thoughts have been in my mind, and perhaps in the minds of many of you. And very mingled they may have been with you, as they have been with me. But the first things, the beginnings, of which I want to speak to you in this letter, are different.

i. Creation. Turn to Genesis i.: "In the beginning God created the heaven and the earth."—made them out of nothing. This infallible history is also stated by John: "In the beginning was the Word, and the Word was with God, and the Word was God. The same was in the beginning with God. All things were made by Him; and without Him was not anything made that was made" (i. 1—3). The Apostle Paul teaches the same truth in Heb. i. 2; and in the same epistle, deals a deadly blow to the evolutionist of to-day by saying, "Through faith we understand that

the worlds were framed by the Word of God, so that
things which are seen were not made of things which
do appear " (xi. 3). There was an originating cause for
the wonderful and beautiful fabric, and the seen
things were not made of things which we now look on,
but by faith we believe that out of nothing all that
now makes up the worlds came, at the divine Word, and
framed by the infinite wisdom of the Creator. Mark
Paul's word as to the how we know that all we see
God made, " through faith." If then an evolutionist
should tell you that the present form of things required
" millions of years " to be what it is, ask him where he
was when God laid the foundations of the earth (Job
xxxviii.), and if he has measured the possibilities of
omnipotence. Then, for your own good, turn to the
beautiful account of the work of making man: " And
God said, Let Us make man in Our own image, after
Our likeness: . . . so God created man in His own
image, in the image of God created He him. And the
Lord God formed man of the dust of the ground, and
breathed into his nostrils the breath of life; and man
became a living soul " (Gen. i. 26, 27; ii. 7). This,
my dear friends, is the infallible history of our origin.
And the men who deny this, and affirm that man came
from *something*, of which, of course, they themselves
know nothing, and *when* they know not, will be found
guilty of making God a liar. Let me refer you to
the words of Moses to the congregation concerning
Korah, Dathan and Abiram, " Depart, I pray you, from
the tents of these wicked men, and touch nothing of
theirs, lest ye be consumed in all their sins " (Num. xvi.
26). So do you depart from the evolutionist. Also I
ask you to read carefully Gen. i. and ii.; Ps. xxxiii. 6;
Jno. i. 3; Acts xvii. 24; Rom. i. 20; Heb. i. 2; xi. 3).

ii. The second beginning is that of sin. To this sad
beginning let us pay close attention. Man was made
in the likeness and image of God. A noble, pure
creature, and a king: said God to him, " Have dominion
over the fish of the sea, and over the fowl of the air,
and over every living thing that moveth upon the

earth." He was wise also: " And out of the ground the Lord God formed every beast of the field, and every fowl of the air, and brought them to Adam to see what he would call them: and whatsoever Adam called every living creature, that was the name thereof " (Gen. i. 28; ii. 19). And God placed Adam under law. Remember that where no law is, there is no transgression. " Sin is the transgression of the law." Adam broke the law, and died, lost the wonderful image in which he was created, and became a sinner. Thus began evil. Thus came ignorance, enmity, unthankfulness, impurity, idolatry, murder, and every hateful thing. Also thus came in mortality, and the suffering, and the diseases which terminate our lives. Write across all trouble, *sin;* doctors might write on every certificate of death, *sin.* Read Rom. v. 12, 13; 1 Cor. xv. 22. Sin began in Eden, where grace does not prevent, it ends in hell.

iii. The next thing I will name to you is the beginning of the gospel. It was opened to fallen Adam in Eden (Gen. iii. 15). It was revealed in different ways to the " Fathers " (Heb. iii. and iv. 2); to Noah, and by him to all who saw him preparing an ark to the saving of his house (Heb. xi. 7). But it began in the full sense of the word when Christ came (Mark i. 1). O, what an opening of the love, wisdom, goodness, grace, and power of God there was in and by Christ when He came, the first-born son of the virgin Mary: " For the law was given by Moses, but grace and truth came by Jesus Christ " (Jno. i. 17); by

" Jesus, God's dear Son,
    Wrapped in humanity."

iv. The fourth beginning for me to mention is the communication of the life of God to a redeemed sinner. This is the new birth. " Ye must be born again," said Christ to Nicodemus. This is the washing of regeneration, the renewing of the soul, the creating work of the Holy Ghost; the beginning of all true experience. Conviction of sin, bondage *felt* under the law, faith, prayer, hope, pardon, all come by Him who came in the fulness of time, was "made of a woman, made under the law, to redeem them that were under the law, that we might receive the adoption of sons" (Gal. iv. 4, 5).

v. The next beginning is the beginning of providence. Divine providence moved Cain and Abel to choose their respective callings, the one chose to be a gardener, and the other decided to be a shepherd. In His judicial providence God scattered the builders of Babel, and confounded their language. In His providence He called Abram out of his own country and led him about. In a word the Bible shows the marvellous movements of God in the nations of the earth, working by whatever means He would. He provided a home and shelter for a time for the Holy Child Jesus in Egypt, saving Him from the rage of Herod (Matt. ii. 12, 13). We are the subjects of God's providence, even if we are ignorant of the fact.

vi. Lastly, for my letter must not exceed proper limits, there will be a beginning of eternity for us. God is the eternal God: past, present, and future, to Him are one eternal now. But to us, as our mortal lives begin, so will our eternity begin (Matt. xxv. 46; Rom. vi. 23). The Lord give us eternal life. "I am the good Shepherd; the good Shepherd giveth His life for the sheep" (Jno. x. 11, 28).

Your affectionate friend,
Brighton, February, 1927. J. K. Popham.

"Remember now thy Creator."

My dear young Friends,—It appears quite suitable that I should, at the opening of the new year, address a few words to you with respect to your position as God's creatures, and what, as such, you owe to Him. And I should like to place at the head of my remarks the solemn and important words given by inspiration of God: "Remember now thy Creator in the days of thy youth" (Eccles. xii. 1).

They are a divine direction, and therefore demand serious and strict attention, the most implicit obedience.

Our being is of vast and undying importance, chiefly because of its relation to God. When "the silver cord is loosed, or the golden bowl is broken, or the pitcher broken at the fountain, or the wheel broken at the cistern, then shall the dust return to the earth as it was, and the spirit shall return to God who gave it" (vers. 6, 7). The greatest and gravest sin man commits is the sin of unbelief; and unbelief is forgetfulness of God.

i. Therefore, *remember that God is your Creator.* In this respect, "He is not far from every one of us; for in Him we live, and move, and have our being." The science which would account for your being in a way that contradicts the account given in Genesis, is "the opposition of science falsely so called" (1 Tim. vi. 20).

ii. *Remember, also, God's sovereign authority over you.* "Man's goings are of the Lord" (Prov. xx. 24). If any of you be thinking that you are your own to dispose of as you please, God grant you may be brought to consider how He reproves you in His Word: "Go to now, ye that say, To-day or to-morrow we will go into such a city, and continue there a year, and buy and sell, and get gain. Whereas ye know not what shall be on the morrow. For what is your life? It is even a vapour, that appeareth for a little time, and then vanisheth away. For that ye ought to say, If the Lord will, we shall live, and do this or that" (James iv. 13—15). If a change in your life seems necessary, if there appears a better prospect for you in another situation or town, seek, as God's creatures, His guidance.

iii. *Remember that your Creator is God only wise.* "O Lord, how manifold are Thy works! In wisdom hast Thou made them all: the earth is full of Thy riches" (Ps. civ. 24). "The Lord by wisdom hath founded the earth: by understanding hath He established the heavens" (Prov. iii. 19). There is doubtless an infinitely wise and good reason in Him for the darkest and most utterly confused circumstances of our short lives. "It is not in man that walketh to direct his steps. His eyes are upon all the ways of the sons of men, to give to everyone according to his ways, and according to the fruit of his doings. O, it is a solemn thing to be under the penetrating gaze of God!

iv. *Remember His power.* No earthly power can work so as to effect good or evil but as ordained or permitted by the Almighty God. When He cast out devils, they must seek and obtain His permission to enter into a herd of swine. When thousands of people were far from their homes, and hungry, in their following Him, He multiplied a few loaves and fishes to appease their hunger. The devouring jaws of lions are locked by God when the safety of His beloved Daniel requires such a miracle. The consuming fire is converted into a pleasant ambient air for the refreshing of God's noble confessors. " Is there anything too hard for the Lord ?" To His own disciples He said, " Fear not them which kill the body, but are not able to kill the soul: but rather fear Him which is able to destroy both body and soul in hell " (Matt. x. 28).

v. *Remember the most righteous claims of God upon you.* These are expressed in the book from which we have before quoted: " Let us hear the conclusion of the whole matter: Fear God, and keep His commandments; for this is the whole duty of man " (Eccles. xii. 13). What the commandments are Jesus told a lawyer: " Jesus said unto him, Thou shalt love the Lord thy God with all thy heart, and with all thy soul, and with all thy mind. This is the first and great commandment. And the second is like unto it: Thou shalt love thy neighbour as thyself " (Matt. xxii. 37—39).

O, but who can do this—that is, *meet the divine claims?* Only One could, and did, even Immanuel. May you, my young friends, be taught by the Spirit what is your duty, and your absolute inability, and that your inability is part of your guilt, and then may you be brought to know that the Lord Jesus obtained eternal redemption for you.

vi. *Remember God's Word.* It was given by inspiration of God; therefore it is infallible, and full of authority. Read it carefully; endeavour to walk according to its holy directions. Do not forget that the greatness of our beloved country is the result of national attention to the Bible. O that the nation may return to its former regard for the sacred Book!

vii. *Remember that you must die, and "stand before the judgment seat of Christ,* that every one may receive the things done in his body, according to that he hath done, whether it be good or bad" (2 Cor. v. 10).

viii. *Remember there is a heaven and a hell to receive men when they die.* You may see these habitations spoken of in the Scriptures.

May the Lord cause you, my dear readers, to consider the above matters. The new year may bring many changes to you; some pleasing, some painful. It may bring *one* and the *last* change—even death. "It is appointed unto man once to die, and after death the judgment."

God be with you, and bless you in all His most wise and holy providence, and give you His grace, if it please Him.   So prays,
               Your affectionate friend,
Brighton, January, 1920.   J. K. POPHAM.

The Mystery of Pain, etc.

1.

My dear young Friends,—It has occurred to me that my time in writing this monthly letter, and yours in reading it, might be well, perhaps usefully, spent, if we consider what one may call a *catch phrase*. It has become common, though probably more used in the religious world than in the profane. Anyhow, I take it as it is used in the religious world, because I fear that some of our own people have been deceived by specious sound. For it appeals more to the imagination than the intellect. The phrase is "the mystery of pain." It sounds very taking, but it won't bear investigation. Let us look at it, analyse it. A mystery is a covered, or hidden thing; it is not necessarily known, but is knowable, yet only by revelation. Thus, while the Lord

spoke to the multitudes in parables, He opened, or
revealed, the mysteries of the kingdom of heaven to His
disciples (Matt. xiii. 11). The word is used to denote
the doctrine of Christ's Person (1 Tim. iii. 16). The
gospel is called the mystery of the faith (1 Tim. iii. 9;
Eph. vi. 19). The Trinity is called a mystery (Col. ii.
2). Also it is the word the Holy Ghost has chosen to
set before us the union which exists between Christ and
the church (Eph. v. 32). And the resurrection is
called a mystery (1 Cor. xv. 52). By the above passages of Scripture it will be obvious that a mystery is
a thing unknown until revealed. Bear that truth in
mind.

Turn now to the word "pain." It is either physical
or mental. When physical it is, generally speaking,
easily diagnosed, and is regarded as a symptom. When
mental it is the result of a shock, or great sorrow; it
has a known cause. The word itself is significant and
explanatory. The dictionary says it is punishment,
from Latin *pœna,* penal; penalty, suffering annexed to
the commission of a crime. "Pain is punishment."*

Here we have two words which singly and etymo-
logically mean, first, something hid which can only be
known by revelation; and second, a well, universally
known thing, if we may call *pain* a "thing." Put
them together and they mean, in plain English, "The
mystery of a well known thing," which is nonsense.

But some will say to me, "O, but the term is used
theologically." Well, be it so. Let us, then, look at
the catching phrase from a theological view-point.
Theology is made up of two words, *Theos,* God, and
logos, discourse. And the dictionary gives the definition
of the word as "The science of divine things." This
puts the taking phrase on the highest plane. On this
plane we will examine it, with all possible brevity.

On the word *mystery* we need say no more. Refer
again to the several passages of the Word of God which
I have noted. Our attention therefore must be given
to the *fact* of "pain." About this there is no mystery.

* Trench on the Study of Words.

It is absolutely clear in the Scripture that pain is the fruit of sin. The entrance of sin into the pure man is indeed a mystery; why the glorious Creator permitted sin to deface His own image in man, and ruin his future race, is one of the secret things which belong to God. But sin having come into our being and ruined us spiritually, intellectually, morally, and physically, pain is an inevitable consequence. Who can fully imagine the pain, the anguish of Adam and Eve on their expulsion from Eden, their first, and erstwhile shameless and thornless home? But there was no mystery about it. It was the fruit of their sin, now terribly brought home to them. What anguish would rend their parental hearts when Cain slew Abel; and what shame would cover them as they reflected on their own disobedience, when they viewed the effects of it in a slain son, and the curse of God on the murderer. What distortion of pain, what moans of anguish do we see and hear in the infallible Book of God in its faithful records of gaunt famine, of loathsome pestilence, of rapine, murder, of the destruction of cities and empires. To mention instances would be to quote the greater part of the Bible. In all these records of pain, shame, and sorrow is there a hint about a mystery? Is it not either a stated or an assumed *fact* that sin is the open cause of all? I really hope you are all too well acquainted with your Bibles to require that I should go any farther by way of proof that sin is the source and procuring cause of pain. What, then, shall I say about the "catch phrase" to which I am asking your attention? Why this, that it clothes a deep heresy; it is an implicit denial of the Fall. And it would fain hide the denial under a term that looks so wise, so innocent. A "mystery," who would profanely uncover it? "pain," whose sympathy is not drawn out? And to the mind that is naturally religious a sort of halo surrounds the pleasing theory. But let us tear away the flimsy cover; let Scripture light chase away the false glamour. Then shall we see the formula to be a hideous heresy, a denial of God's Word, a revelation of extreme and awful ignorance in those who adopt and use it. It is a serious misnomer, possible to those, and only those, who are led by the god of this world. Some may use it without thinking of its import, carried away by a sound.

One reflection I would make here. It is of "immense importance that we use such names for things as shall not involve or suggest an error."* May this word be of use to you. As you grow into manhood and woman-hood you may have many an occasion to prove the importance and value of accuracy in the use of words and terms. And above all be careful in your acceptance of terms used to express divine truths. Often, as in the case before us, a stone may be given you for bread, a scorpion for an egg, a serpent for a fish.

God be with you and about you in His wise and holy providence, cause you to watch His hand, and to acknowledge Him in all your ways, and be with and in you to save you eternally.

So prays,
Your affectionate friend,
Brighton, May, 1922.   J. K. POPHAM.

2.

My dear young Friends,—In my last letter I en-deavoured to expose the fallacy of the catch phrase, "The mystery of pain," and showed from the Word of God that pain is punishment, and that that infallible Book does not cover, or make, a mystery of pain. It is distinctly the outcome of sin. Sin must be followed by suffering punishment in some form. The nature of God, and the terms of the covenant of works demand this. God can by no means clear the guilty. To imagine that the mercy of God will not permit Him to punish sin discovers a deplorable, God-dishonouring ignorance of Him. And this ignorance is common to all men. "Vain man would be wise, though man be born like a wild ass's colt." And in his supposed and vaunted wisdom vain man thinks God to be altogether such an

* Trench on the Study of Words.

one as himself. O ignorance extreme! But, though it is perfectly clear from Scripture that pain is punishment, and there is no mystery about that sad fact, let us not think there is no mystery connected with sin, or in many of God's dealings with men because of their sins. As I said in my last letter, the beginning or entrance of sin is a mystery. Deep, solemn, and inscrutable to us is that mystery. It is unsearchable to all creatures; it is one of God's matters, of which He giveth no account. We believe He is righteous in all His works and ways; but when He covers Himself or any of His works with clouds and darkness, silent reverence becomes all creatures. For when He makes darkness His " pavilion round about Him, dark waters, and thick clouds of the skies," it is presumption to arraign Him at the bar of human reason.

There is sometimes a mystery in the manner of God's dealings both in the church and the world. Wicked men have often been used to punish His people for sin. A notable instance of this we see in Assyria being sent against Israel. The Assyrian was the rod of His anger, and the staff in his hand was the manifestation of His indignation; yet the motive of Assyria was not to do the bidding of God, but just to gratify their lust of conquest; and when the work of chastisement was accomplished, the rod was broken and the stout heart of the king of Assyria punished (Isa. x.). Jealousy, cruel as the grave, was employed by the All-wise Sovereign Lord to send Joseph into Egypt to bring to pass His own merciful ends. To this Joseph bore testimony in the magnanimous consolation he gave his humbled brethren: " Now therefore be not grieved nor angry with yourselves that ye sold me hither: for God did send me before you to preserve life. And God sent me before you to preserve you a posterity in the earth, and to save your lives by a great deliverance " (Gen. xlv. 5, 7). In all that singular providence there was a majesty in the divine permission of sin, and the use God made of the murderous design of Jacob's ungracious sons in preparing the way for the accomplishment of the predicted sojourn and affliction of the Israelites in Egypt. By the divinely permitted persecution of the church in Jerusalem, the saints were scattered abroad and went everywhere, preaching the Word throughout the regions of Judea and Samaria, and by the foolishness of preaching the Lord saved them who, through grace, believed. In this instance, as in a countless number of other instances, the Lord God Omnipotent reigned, and frustrated the tokens of the father of lies, and made the arch diviner mad, turned him backward, and made his knowledge foolish, saying to Jerusalem, which is above, Thou shalt be inhabited with converts who shall be called with an invincible call by the preaching of these persecuted saints. By death the Lord took away the youthful and promising king, Edward VI., and permitted the bigoted, persecuting Mary to succeed him. Human reason, affection and unbelief, probably in many, questioned the wisdom and love of God in allowing the Reformation to be put back. But how illustriously did His grace shine in the martyrs of Jesus who loved not their lives unto the death, and who overcame by the blood of the Lamb! Wondrously, gloriously has the God of all grace turned the lapses, the backslidings of His people to a good account! Each chastened son unites with R. Erskine, sorrowfully and gladly singing:

" Sin for my good shall work and win,
But 'tis not good for me to sin."

The Scriptures, which are written for our learning, contain accounts of the falls of eminent saints, and display the glory of God's grace in restoring them. Particulars I need not enter into, you can refer to the cases.

There is, then, mystery in the dealings of God with men on account of sin. Many of them are left on record to be examples and warnings to the Lord's people. Happy are they to whom such solemn examples are made effectual by the Holy Ghost (1 Cor. x.).

Your affectionate friend,

Brighton, June, 1922.   J. K. POPHAM.

The Significations of "World."

My dear young Friends,—This letter is to be about the word "world." It is a very great and important word. It affects us, as we are in it, in some of the senses in which it is used in Scripture; it influences us, and we influence it, as a stone thrown into water makes a ring which multiplies into many rings: "For none of us liveth to himself, and no man dieth to himself" (Rom. xiv. 7).

The term "world" is used variously in the infallible Word. Of course, the different senses will occur to you. (a) It is used to express creation-work (Gen. i. 1, 2; Jno. i. 10; Heb. i. 2). The divinely inspired words kill and bury evolution. No man will ever make that God-dishonouring system a living truth. And, received by faith, these words settle the mind (Heb. xi. 3). It is because men do not like to retain God in their knowledge that they are given over to a reprobate mind, and are blinded to the clear and indelible impression of the eternal power and Godhead which is on the creation of the world (Rom. i. 20, 28). Oh, stand fast by the world as created in the beginning by the Son of God!

(b) The Word of God tells us that the world stands for fallen mankind: "By one man sin entered into the world, and death by sin, and so death passed upon all men, for that all have sinned" (Rom. v. 12). Here we all are; no man can claim exemption; "As in Adam all die" (1 Cor. xv. 22). The whole of this fallen world lieth in wickedness (1 Jno. v. 19). What a terrible state to "lie in"! For Christ says wickedness is an abomination to His lips (Prov. viii. 8). He cannot bear those who are evil. This world has its own evil course, according to which all walk by nature (Eph. ii. 2). These men love darkness rather than light because their deeds are evil (Jno. iii. 19). This "world" is enmity against God, and sometimes He chases wicked men out of it, deals in open judgment and vindicates His most righteous character (Job xviii. 18). For this "world" the Lord Jesus prays not (Jno. xvii. 9). Could a more terrible evil fall on a sinner than not to

be prayed for by Christ! The solemnity of it, the
authority of it, the eternity of the evil! The everlasting
woe of that " I pray not for the world "! Oh who,
feeling to be by nature a child of wrath, and in the
world that lieth in wickedness, does not, at the sight
and feeling of such a word, cry to the Lord for a manifested, an enjoyed interest, in the blessed word, " I pray
for them " ? An all-covering prayer, an everlastingly
inclusive prayer! In it is redemption.

> " Safety on earth, and after death
> The plenitude of heaven."

(c) The word is used to set forth the objects of God's
love. " For God so loved the world that He gave His
only begotten Son, that whosoever believeth in Him
should not perish, but have everlasting life. In this was
manifested the love of God toward us, because that
God sent His only begotten Son into the world that we
might live through Him. Herein is love, not that we
loved God, but that He loved us, and sent His Son to
be the propitiation for our sins " (Jno. iii. 16; 1 Jno.
iv. 9, 10). Much controversy has there been about the
above words, but a little attention to the context, and
the *nature* of the atonement will settle every unprejudiced
mind, while to the regenerated sinner they are a wonderful plea. How fervently he desires to be relieved
of his burden of guilt by the efficacious blood of Christ,
and thus realise an interest in His propitiatory sacrifice,
and go forth unto Him without the camp of the world
both religious and profane (Heb. xiii. 12—14).

(d) The world is set in opposition to the church.
" And now come I to Thee: and these things I speak
in the world, that they might have My joy fulfilled in
themselves. I have given them Thy Word; and the
world hath hated them, because they are not of the
world, even as I am not of the world. I pray not that
Thou shouldest take them out of the world, but that
Thou shouldest keep them from the evil. They are
not of the world, even as I am not of the world " (Jno.
xvii. 13—16). This most positive word is very search-

ing and discriminating. Your chosen and constant company will declare your heart and affection. If the world is your choice, then you love it, and cannot, in that unregenerate state, serve God. "Ye cannot serve two masters;" they issue different orders and commands. If you are friends of this world, you are enemies of God (Matt. vi. 24; Jas. iv. 4). The vanities of the world are too glaring, too pronounced, too openly opposed to Scripture to be unknown. Yet some of them have got in among us. It is said that ninety-nine out of every hundred of the women and girls of this nation have cut off their natural glory, and wear short, or bobbed hair. Also we see the immodest short dress, and low neck. Ought there to be such an open disregard of God's Word? (1 Cor. xi. 14, 16; 1 Tim. ii. 9). I entreat those of you, my young female readers, who may thoughtlessly have fallen into the unseemly fashions, or who may be entertaining the intention of following them, to consider the Word of God, to shrink from the dishonour you have done yourselves (or from the half-formed purpose). The Lord help you.

(e) The utter insufficiency, emptiness, and vanity of the whole world as contrasted with the reality, worth, need, and immortality of the soul, the Scripture declares (Matt. xvi. 26; Ps. xlix. 6—15; Luke xii. 15—21).

God grant that the above words of Holy Scripture may be made the words of God *in* your hearts, that thus you may rightly consider your position, your state before Him, and your latter end (Deut. xxxii. 29; Ps. xxxix. 4; and cause each of you to cry out, "What must I do to be saved?" (Acts xvi. 30.)

Your affectionate friend,
Brighton, October, 1926.   J. K. POPHAM.

"Rain," "Water," etc.

1.

My dear young Friends,—I am disposed to call your attention to the immense blessing God gives to men in sending rain from heaven. Indeed, it is spoken of as a

witness for Himself, as the living God, who "left not
Himself without witness, in that He did good, and gave
us rain from heaven, and fruitful seasons, filling our
hearts with food and gladness" (Acts xiv. 17). Rain is
a necessity of life, so it is one of the most beneficent
gifts of God to man. How barren would our fields be
without it; how would the cattle languish! And what
would become of our great cities and towns without the
cleansing, refreshing showers heaven's bounty gives?
Yet, the constancy and sufficiency of the blessing
deadens our minds to our dependence on its ever-
bountiful Giver. By a grievous famine He made Israel
know both their sin and dependence (Jer. xiv.).

Rain is a fertilizer. To Israel, God gave it as a token
of His acceptance of their diligent observance of His
commandments, in their national covenant. "And it
shall come to pass, if ye shall hearken diligently unto
My commandments which I command you this day, to
love the Lord your God, and to serve Him with all your
heart, and with all your soul, that I will give you the
rain of your land in his due season, the first rain and
the latter rain, that thou mayest gather in thy corn, and
thy wine, and thine oil" (Deut. xi. 13, 14). The "first
rain" is the "rain of thy seed, that thou shalt sow the
ground withal" (Isa. xxx. 23).

Disobedience brought drought. "And if ye will not
for all this (previous judgment) hearken unto Me, then
will I punish you seven times more for your sins. And
I will break the pride of your power; and I will make
your heaven as iron, and your earth as brass. And
your strength shall be spent in vain: for your land shall
not yield her increase, neither shall the trees of the land
yield their fruits" (Lev. xxvi. 18—20).

It will occupy you well to look out the scriptures
which show that drought was often sent as a punishment for national sin.

On the other hand, God sometimes used this bounty
of His as a punishment by sending it in such quantity
as to be ruinous. "He causeth it to come whether for
correction" ("a rod," margin), as the "great rain of

His strength" (Job xxxvii. 6, 13). Such was the flood whereby the world was drowned.

Then, *rain is spoken of metaphorically.* i. In a gracious sense. "Give ear, O ye heavens, and I will speak; and hear, O earth, the words of My mouth. My doctrine shall drop as the rain, My speech shall distil as the dew, as the small rain upon the tender herb, and as the showers upon the grass" (Deut. xxxii. 1, 2). This most gracious and sovereign promise is fulfilled in the election of grace, when Christ comes down as rain upon mown grass, as showers that water the earth (Ps. lxxii. 6). God grant that you, my friends, may be favoured with hunger and thirst after righteousness, then you will one day receive the refreshing, reviving rain of pardon, peace and joy.

ii. *Rain is spoken of in the sense of solemn and overwhelming judgments of God on the ungodly.* Concerning Gog, who came into the land of Israel, God said, "And I will plead against him with pestilence and with blood: and I will rain upon him, and upon his bands, and upon the many people that are with him, an overflowing rain, and great hailstones, fire and brimstone." "Upon the wicked He shall rain snares, fire and brimstone, and an horrible tempest: this shall be the portion of their cup" (Ezek. xxxviii. 22; Ps. xi. 6).

No wicked person shall be able to avoid this fearful storm. The rain descends, the floods come, and the winds blow, and beat upon all who are not built upon the Rock, and great will be the ruin which will swallow them up (Matt. vii. 26).

What an infinite mercy it would be for us, if the doctrines of sovereign, electing love, grace, regeneration, justification and sanctification should rain upon us!

Your affectionate friend and well-wisher,
Brighton, July, 1921. J. K. POPHAM.

2.

My dear young Friends,—On June 13th the King opened London's new Reservoir at Littleton, near Laleham, Middlesex. It forms an important part of

the Metropolitan Water Board's scheme for improving
the water supply of London. The basin is nearly 800
acres in area. When the basin is filled—an operation
which, it is estimated, will take about three months—it
will contain 6,750,000,000 gallons of water to a depth
of about 40ft. A cost of £2,145,364 has been involved
in its construction, and to make room for the reservoir,
part of the village of Littleton was demolished, while
the River Ash at one point had to be diverted. In an
address to the King, Mr. C. G. Musgrave, chairman of
the Board, said that, when filled, the reservoir could
provide anchorage for a fleet of battleships. It is larger
than all the other Thames Valley reservoirs put together, and will hold enough water to supply the
capital's seven million inhabitants for a month. *The
Times* contains an exceedingly interesting article on
London's water supply, with which many rulers of
England have been directly or indirectly associated.
" It was Henry III. who, in 1236, granted liberty to
the citizens of London to bring water from Tyburn to
the city through leaden pipes. Of this period, though a
little later, a surviving relic is the name of Lamb's
Conduit Street, in Bloomsbury. Tyburn, the name of
a small stream, now running underground from Hamp-
stead through Regent's Park and Green Park to the
Thames at Westminster." It was at Tyburn that felons
were hanged. The gallows stood at the junction of the
Edgware and Bayswater Roads. In 1759 the permanent
structure was replaced by a movable gallows, the
original site being occupied by the new turnpike house.

Reflect on this. Water brought into the city of
London from Tyburn through leaden pipes! In 1236
the conducting—or conduit—of water in the above
manner was possibly regarded as a triumph of engineering skill. Contrast that work with building of vast
reservoirs for storing, and the underground structures
for distributing, the essential supply of water to the
City proper, and to London's teeming millions. Think
of the expert knowledge required to weigh and measure
the volume of water to be contained in one place! The

foundations must bear the weight of 6,750,000,000 gallons of water, the walls must resist the pressure of the vast body! And all this human skill is required for the health of our Babylon, in the midst of which are some of the sons of Zion.

But we are not to think that engineering is of recent birth. To go back no farther than king Hezekiah, who lived seven hundred years before Christ, we learn from the sacred, inspired record that there was considerable knowledge of that science in his day. It is said that " he made a pool, and a conduit, and brought water into the city." " This same Hezekiah also stopped the upper water course of Gihon, and brought it straight down to the west side of the city " (2 Kings xx. 20; 2 Chron. xxxii. 30). Particular notice is here taken of the aqueduct, as amongst the greatest of Hezekiah's works. " In exploring the subterranean channel conveying the water from Virgin's Forest to Siloam, I discovered a similar channel entering from the north, a few yards from its commencement; and on tracing it up near the Mugrabin Gate, where it became so choked with rubbish that it could be traversed no further, I there found it turned to the west, in the direction of the south end of the cleft, or saddle of Zion; and if this channel was not constructed for the purpose of conveying the waters of Hezekiah's aqueduct, I am unable to suggest any purpose to which it could have been applied. Perhaps the reason why it was not brought down on the Zion side was that Zion was already well watered in its lower portion by the Great Pool, 'the lower pool of Gihon.' And accordingly Williams' ' Holy City ' renders this passage, ' He stopped the upper outflow of the waters of Gihon ' " (Barclay's " City of the Great King," cf. Robinson's " Biblical Researches," Porter's " Handbook," Hardy's " Notices of the Holy Land "). The construction of this aqueduct required not only masonic, but engineering skill; for the passage was bored through a continuous mass of rock. Hezekiah's pool or reservoir, made to receive the water within the north-west part of the city, still exists.

From the above we may make two obvious reflections. i. The necessity of water for the health of cities. ii. The mercy of God not only in providing so plentifully that essential element, but also in giving knowledge and skill to men to overcome natural difficulties to supply the need. We draw our water, we fill our baths morning by morning, and perhaps seldom thank the beneficent Giver, or think of the engineering skill which has brought it into our houses through mountains, hills and valleys. The cities of Liverpool and Manchester are largely supplied with water from Welsh rivers and lakes, many miles distant. Even where there is plenty we should not waste water.

A word in conclusion. Is water so necessary to our existence, to the well-being of our villages, towns, and cities? so necessary that millions are spent to provide us with it? Is God so good to us as to provide sufficient for all? How necessary for the eternal good of men is the river of water of life! And how amazing is the provision, the very Son of God in our nature, full of grace and truth. And what wisdom is manifested in bringing the rich provision to a sinner, even the Holy Ghost, who gives life, hunger, thirst to all in whom He is " a well of water, springing up into everlasting life." A famine of water may come, has often come, to a land; see the famines told of in the Bible. But to souls thirsting for the river of water of life no famine will come. There may not always be the plentiful supply the soul desires, but the river of God is full of water. God give us thirst for it, and then quench our thirst by it!

Your affectionate friend,

Brighton, August, 1925.   J. K. POPHAM.